post- Dykes To Watch Out For

by Alison Bechdel

Firebrand Books

Alison Bechdel's cartoons appear regularly in more than sixty publications internationally.

Cover Design by Tom Devlin

Printed in the United States by McNaughton & Gunn

Library of Congress Cataloging-in-Publication Data

Bechdel, Alison
Post-dykes to watch out for / by Alison Bechdel.
p. cm.
ISBN 1-56341-123-7 (cloth) -- ISBN 1-56341-122-9 (paper)
1. Lesbians -- United States -- Comic books, strips, etc.
2. Lesbianism -- United States -- Comic books, strips, etc. 3. American wit and humor, Pictorial.
I. Title.
HQ75.6.U5B4245 2000
306.76'63'0207--dc21 00-039323
CIP

for Nancy Bereano

Thanks to Trissa Baden, Helen Bechdel, Deb Lashman, Samuel Lurie, Will Marquess, Cati Marsh, Paula Myrick, Alissa Oppenheimer, Lynette Reep, Nan Reid, Esther Rothblum, Morgan Shore, Sarah Van Arsdale, Joannie Wales, and Meg "Copy Goddess" Wallace. A huge tip o' the nib to Cathy Resmer for her multifarious modes of support. And to Amy Rubin, for aiding and abetting everything in this book, my most effusive gratitude.

WHEN WE LAST LOOKED IN, SOME OF OUR SUBJECTS HAD VEERED A BIT TOO CLOSE TO THE RIM OF THAT VAST CAULDRON OF PROCESSED CHEESE SPREAD OTHERWISE KNOWN AS THE GREAT AMERICAN MELTING POT.

MEANWHILE, HOUSEMATES **GINGER**, **SPARROW**, AND **LOIS** ARE ABOUT TO SET THE COMMUNAL LIVING ENDURANCE RECORD... AND THEY'RE SIGNING ON FOR ANOTHER HITCH!

THEIR COMMUNE EXPANDS BY ONE WHEN **STUART**, SPARROW'S NEW, RATHER MASCULINE PARAMOUR, NEEDS NEW DIGS.

After a disheartening stint on the job market, Ginger accepts a position in the English Department of Buffalo Lake State College...

Sparrow runs the local battered women's shelter...

...And Lois continues to hone her marketing expertise at that august emporium of the printed word and other sundries, **MADWIMMIN BOOKS.**

Sales have been languishing at Madwimmin, where boss **JEZANNA** and humble clerk **MO** pluckily staff the barricades against the corporate blitzkrieg.

MO'S OFF-DUTY LIFE HAS BEEN FRAUGHT WITH FINANCIAL SUSPENSE AS WELL, EVER SINCE SHE BECAME AFFILIATED WITH **SYDNEY**, WOMEN'S STUDIES PROFESSOR AND WORLD CLASS SPENDTHRIFT.

NEVER RELUCTANT TO SOLVE THE PROBLEMS OF OTHERS, MO PROPOSES COHABITATION...

...AND SYDNEY MOVES IN, LOCK, STOCK, AND TENURE TRACK.

WILL MO COME TO HER SENSES?

WILL MADWIMMIN BOOKS GO THE WAY OF FULL-SERVICE GAS?

WILL CLARICE, TONI, AND RAFFI RETAIN THEIR DISTINCTIVE TEXTURES, OR BE ASSIMILATED WHOLESALE INTO THE AMERICAN CHEESE FONDUE?

PONY UP FOR THE DAMN BOOK ALREADY AND FIND OUT.

Enough Already

298

GET OUT YOUR ROLODEX. AS WE REJOIN OUR WANDERING NARRATIVE, THERE SEEM TO BE A FEW CHANGES OF ADDRESS.

CLARICE AND TONI HAVE EMIGRATED TO THE RIGHT SIDE OF THE TRACKS.

SYDNEY HAS BECOME MO'S NOT-SO-DOMESTIC PARTNER.

JEZANNA, IN A GRUDGING ACT OF FILIAL DUTY, HAS OPENED UP HER HOME TO HER BEREAVED FATHER.

AND IN A QUASI-MARRIAGE OF CONVENIENCE, STUART HAS TAKEN LODGINGS WITH SPARROW AND THE GIRLS.

RAFFI'S BEEN MANIFESTING SOME CURIOUS NEW TRAITS SINCE KINDERGARTEN BEGAN.

AT MADWIMMIN BOOKS, MO'S SHOWING THE ROPES TO SOPHIE, THE NEW INTERN.

GINGER'S NEW JOB AT BUFFALO LAKE STATE IS SURPASSING HER EXPECTATIONS.

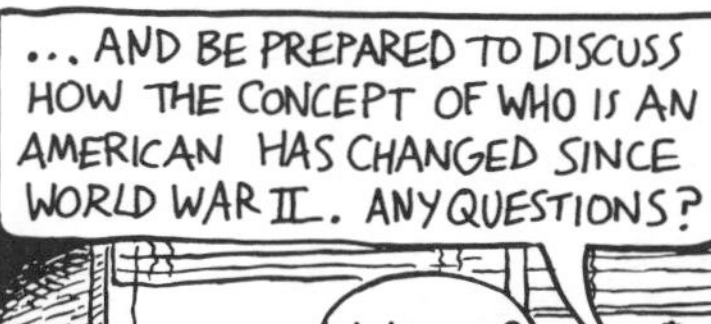

The BIRTH of OUTRAGE

300

MO'S MATER-FAMILIAS RINGS UP DURING BUSINESS HOURS.

WHAT IS IT ABOUT THE MATTHEW SHEPARD MURDER? QUEERS HAVE BEEN GETTING BASHED AND KILLED FOR **EONS** AND NOBODY BLINKED!
DAILY CORONARY
G.O.P. KILLS HATE CRIMES BILL

NOW ALL OF A SUDDEN WE'RE LAPEL RIBBON OF THE WEEK! EVERYONE'S APPALLED!
UH... DON'T WORRY. NOT QUITE EVERYONE.
ANTI-GAY VIOLENCE UP 81% IN NYC
EX-GAY ADS MOVE TO TV
FRATERNITY MOCKS SHEPARD ATTACK

WAIT. YOU'RE, LIKE, ANGRY BECAUSE PEOPLE ARE REACTING THE WAY THEY SHOULD?
NO! I'M THRILLED THEY GET IT. IT JUST PISSES ME OFF FOR ALL THE TIMES THEY DIDN'T. I MEAN, WHY NOW?

IS IT BECAUSE THE ATTACK WAS SO VICIOUS? BECAUSE YEARS OF ACTIVISM ARE FINALLY PAYING OFF? BECAUSE HE WAS A CLEAN-CUT COLLEGE KID AND NOT A DRAG QUEEN?

GOD! YOU'RE ANALYZING IT LIKE IT'S A CHESS GAME! WHERE'S YOUR RAGE AT THE KILLERS? WHERE'S YOUR RAGE AT THE PARENTS AND POLITICIANS AND PREACHERS WHO TAUGHT THEM TO HATE?
SOPHIE, I'VE BEEN FILLED WITH RAGE SINCE YOU WERE A TWINKLE IN YOUR SPERM DONOR'S EYE.
CONSERVATIVE ESTIMATE.

buyer's remorse
©1998 BY ALISON BECHDEL

ONE AUTUMNAL TUESDAY EVE...
WELL, THAT WAS UNPLEASANT. BUT IT HAD TO BE DONE.
OH, THANKS, LOIS! SINCE GINGER STARTED HER NEW JOB, THE DOG SHIT'S REALLY BEEN PILING UP OUT THERE.
NOV
301

UH... I WASN'T CLEANING UP THE YARD. I JUST CAME FROM THE POLLS.
MMM. THAT WAS A NASTY BUSINESS.
CHEESE
MILK
EE-RUNNING

MAY THE LORD HAVE MERCY ON MY SOUL. I VOTED FOR EVERY MARGINALLY LESSER EVIL ON THE TICKET.
YEAH, ME TOO. AND I'M GETTING PRETTY SICK OF THIS ROTTEN TWO-PARTY DEAL. IT'S GOT TO GO.
10% TRIB

MAYBE IT'LL FINALLY HAPPEN, NOW THAT CLINTON'S TOTALLED THE DEMOCRATS, AND THE REPUBLICANS ARE LOST SOMEWHERE BETWEEN LEVITICUS AND THE 19TH CENTURY.
ARF?
I DON'T KNOW. I'M LOSING FAITH IN PEOPLE'S COMMON SENSE. LIKE, WILL YOU EXPLAIN TO ME WHAT THESE LESBIAN AND GAY GROUPS ARE DOING IN BED WITH CONSERVATIVE REPUBLICANS?
ORGANIC COW
HRC ENDORSES ANTI-CHOICE D'AMATO
"WE'D RATHER HAVE GAYS IN THE MILITARY THAN GUN CONTROL"
QUICHE
EGGS

GETTING REAMED. BUT THEY SEEM TO LIKE IT.
HELLO!
LOG CABIN CLUB VOWS TO DEFEAT TWO LESBIAN CONGRESSIONAL CANDIDATES

HEY, SPARROW. HOW'D THE CLOSING GO THIS MORNING?
WE GOT IT! GINGER AND I OFFICIALLY OWN THE HOUSE!
WELL, I JUST HOPE YOU WON'T TAKE ADVANTAGE OF A SIMPLE PEASANT LAD WITH YOUR DEBAUCHED, LANDED GENTRY WAYS.

LATER, AFTER GINGER RETURNS...
TO OUR NEW HOME. CHEERS.
PROSIT.
SKOAL.
FEH!

UH... GREAT NON-ALCOHOLIC WINE, SPARROW. AUSTERE, YET MEAGER, WITH A HINT OF WELCH'S AND A SOBER FINISH.
HEY, WHAT'S THAT PILE OF SAWDUST UNDER THE WINDOW? I THOUGHT WE CLEANED UP AFTER THE ELECTRICIAN.
WE DID.

WEIRD. MAYBE THE FAMILY RESEARCH COUNCIL CAME BY AND PLANTED A LISTENING DEVICE.
WELL, IT'S DEFINITELY SOME KIND OF BUG. I CAN HEAR IT CHEWING.

MO AND SYDNEY DECIDE TO SPEND THE FIRST HALF OF THEIR CHRISTMAS VACATION WITH SYDNEY'S FATHER AND STEP-MOTHER.

AND THE SECOND HALF WITH MO'S FAMILY.

DAD! I CAN'T **BE-LIEVE** YOU! HAVEN'T I EXPLAINED A THOUSAND TIMES HOW BUNNS AND NOODLE IS **RAPING** THE **CULTURAL LANDSCAPE!?**

THE DRIVE HOME IS A BIT TENSE...

MEANWHILE, THEIR CAT-SITTERS ARE MAKING AN INTERESTING DISCOVERY.

303

IT'S NEW YEAR'S EVE. MO AND SYDNEY HAVE JUST RETURNED FROM VISITING THEIR FAMILIES, AND IN CONSEQUENCE ARE FEELING A BIT FRACTIOUS.

OH, COME ON! YOU'RE NOT GONNA TELL MO! MAYBE SHE ALREADY KNOWS. MAYBE THEY HAVE AN ARRANGEMENT.
AND IT'S NOT LIKE IT'S A **REAL** AFFAIR.
WHAT'S NOT LIKE IT'S A REAL AFFAIR?

OH, LOIS... WE WERE JUST DISCUSSING, UH... IN A PURELY THEORETICAL WAY... WHETHER AN ONLINE AFFAIR COUNTS.
'COUNTS?' SPARROW, YOU'RE SO 20TH CENTURY.

SOON...
HI, KIDS! WELCOME BACK! HOW'RE THE FOLKS?
UNH.
MPH.

OKAY! TONIGHT'S TOPIC: EXTRA-CURRICULAR SEX— IS IT CHEATING IF IT'S ONLY VIRTUAL?
LOIS! WHY DON'T YOU SEE IF ANYONE WANTS MORE HORSERADISH REMOULADE!
OF COURSE IT'S CHEATING! IT WOULD BE A DIVERSION OF EMOTIONAL ENERGY.

I WOULDN'T CALL IT CHEATING. IT'S MORE LIKE REMOTE, INTERACTIVE MASTURBATION.
HMM... HAS SHE BEEN DOING A LOT OF "ON-LINE RESEARCH" LATELY, MO?

OW! JESUS, SPARROW!
WHOOPS.
DARN. THAT WAS SOME TASTY REMOULADE.

leadership vacuum

304

I MISS THE GOOD OLD DAYS. SMASH THE FAMILY! SMASH THE STATE!

WHAT ABOUT CLARICE AND TONI AND RAFFI? D'YOU WANT TO SMASH THEIR FAMILY?
TOM'S of FINLAND
PLEASE, SYDNEY. I'M EXPRESSING AN IDEOLOGICAL CONVICTION, I'M NOT TALKING ABOUT REAL PEOPLE.

MEANWHILE, GINGER'S PREPARING FOR TRASH DAY.
SPARROW, COULDN'T YOU GUYS DISPOSE OF THIS CONTRACEPTIVE DEBRIS MORE DISCREETLY? IT'S REALLY GROSS.
OH, AND YOUR BLOODY TAMPONS AREN'T?
SPERMEX
LIFE STYLE

I DON'T HAVE MY PERIOD. THOSE MUST BE LOIS'S. OR **YOURS.**

!
FLIP!

Z
?
APPOINTMENTS

MEANWHILE, DOWN AT THE LOCAL PHARMACY...

OH. UH... HI, STUART.
UM... HI THERE.
CHECK OUT
VAGICORP YEAST-B-GONE
RHOID OINTMENT

ER... I'M JUST RUNNING AN ERRAND FOR A... A FRIEND. YEAH.
I HEARD THIS STUFF MAKES A GREAT, UH... WINTER WEIGHT CHAIN LUBE, IF YOU BIKE IN THE SNOW.
METAMUCIL

GOD. COULD WE POSSIBLY BE BUYING ANYTHING MORE EMBARRASSING?
LICE EGG REMOVER? AN ENEMA, MAYBE?

HEY, PHUONG! GET ME A PRICE ON THE "MAYBE BABY" PREGNANCY TEST!
JEEZ, THEY SHOULD HAVE PRIVATE CHECK-OUT BOOTHS IN THESE PLACES. LOOK AT THAT POOR LADY!
NICOTINE
V.D.
SUCROSE

THAT'S NO LADY! THAT'S...
SPARROW?

AND WE COULD CONVERT THE UPSTAIRS PORCH INTO AN EXTRA ROOM...
I'LL GLUE GLOW-IN-THE DARK STARS ON THE CEILING. KIDS LOVE THAT. AND WE'LL HAVE TO GET A GATE FOR THE STAIRS, AND PUT THOSE LITTLE COVERS OVER ALL THE ELECTRICAL OUTLETS...

Gossip Failure
©1999 BY ALISON BECHDEL
307

HEY! GUESS WHO'S PICKING UP A FEW PREGNANCY TESTS!
Pillzapoppin' Rx
1156
ANNUAL Truss SALE! % OFF
DON'T FORGET VALENTINE'S DAY
...THIS IS JERRI GROSZ WITH FRESH HAIR.

SPARROW.
TODAY I'LL BE TALKING WITH A GAY MAN IN THE ENTERTAINMENT INDUSTRY...

HOW DID YOU KNOW?
GINGER JUST TOLD ME.
... TO WHOSE EVERY THROAT-CLEARING I WILL RESPOND WITH A COQUETTISH TITTER.

OKAY, BABE. LATER.
GOD, I HATE THAT PHONE.
... AND LATER IN THE HOUR, DAVID BEYONDCOOLGUY WILL EXPLORE THE DANTESQUE IMAGERY OF "TOUCHED BY AN ANGEL."

SHORTLY...
MORNING, JEZ! HEY, GUESS WHO I JUST SAW AT THE DRUGSTORE SHOPPING FOR PREGNANCY TESTS!
MADWIMMIN BOOKS
OPEN

MO, I DON'T HAVE TIME FOR YOUR FOOLISHNESS. THE BOOK BUSINESS IS CONSOLIDATING FASTER THAN THERMONUCLEAR FUSION, AND I'VE GOT A STORE TO KEEP SOLVENT.
GOD! TAKE A BREAK ONCE IN A WHILE! YOU ACT LIKE THE FUTURE OF DEMOCRACY RESTS ON YOUR SHOULDERS.
BUNNS & NOODLE BUYS LEADING WHOLESALE SUPPLIER TO INDEPENDENT BOOKSTORES

YOU THINK IT DOESN'T? JUST WAIT TILL THOUSANDS OF DIVERSE, LOVINGLY TENDED INDEPENDENT BOOKSTORES GET REPLACED BY GENERIC CHAINS, SUBLITERATE **BEAN COUNTER** DOWN AT CORPORATE HQ SELECTING ALL THE TITLES!
OFFICE
INDEPENDENTS PROTEST TO JUSTICE DEPT.
YOU CAN SAY GOODBYE TO BOOKS BY RISKY OR UNPROVEN AUTHORS, LIKE THE ONES I'VE BEEN HANDSELLING OUR CUSTOMERS FOR YEARS. WE'LL ALL BE UP TO OUR **CEREBRAL CORTEXES** IN "CELINE DION'S **TITANIC CHEESECAKE RECIPES!**"
OFFICE
"IT'S LIKE WENDY'S HAVING TO RELY ON McDONALD'S TO SELL THEM FRENCH FRIES."

AND DON'T COME WHINING TO ME ABOUT THE FUTURE OF DEMOCRACY WHEN NO ONE WILL PUBLISH YOUR **SCATHING INDICTMENT** OF THE BOOK INDUSTRY!
OKAY, OKAY! I'M ON YOUR SIDE! DON'T GET YOUR JOCKEYS IN A KNOT.
OFFIC
"EAT OUR DUST JACKETS," CHORTLES BUNNS & NOODLE

A BIT LATER...
WELL, LOOK WHO'S SLUMMING! WHAT BRINGS YOU THREE IN FROM THE LAND OF CHEMLAWN?
NICE TO SEE THE INCREASED COMPETITION HASN'T AFFECTED YOUR CUSTOMER RELATIONS SKILLS.
WE JUST STOPPED IN TO HEAR THE LATEST DISH... ER, I MEAN, TO SUPPORT OUR LOCAL INDEPENDENT BOOKSELLER.

WELL, HAVE I GOT SOME NEWS FOR YOU. GUESS WHO WAS RECENTLY SPOTTED PURCHASING A HOME PREGNANCY TEST!
HARRIET! I KNOW! ISN'T IT WONDERFUL?!

HARRIET? MY HARRIET?
UH... IT'S BEEN 7 YEARS, BABE. I THINK THE STATUTE OF LIMITATIONS HAS RUN OUT ON USE OF THE POSSESSIVE.

pestered

308

SPARROW AND STUART RETURN HOME TOGETHER AFTER A CHANCE ENCOUNTER AT THE DRUG-STORE.

GOD! JUST LEAVE ME ALONE, ALL OF YOU!

DON'T BE ALARMED. MOOD SWINGS ARE A NORMAL PART OF PREGNANCY.
SLAM
STOMP
STOMP
A BABY! GOD, I DON'T KNOW IF I'M READY TO BE A FATHER.
YEAH, ME EITHER.

MAYBE BABY

SHORTLY...
OH MY GOD!

HEY!

I GOT MY PERIOD!
YOU DID?
ARE YOU SURE?
WELL, THAT WAS AN INTERESTING LITTLE ROLLER-COASTER RIDE.
TERMITES AND YOU
PEST

UH... SO IS THAT A NO ON THE ROACH SPECIAL, THEN?
YEAH. BUT IF YOU'RE EVER RUNNING A DEAL ON SPER-MICIDE, GIVE US A CALL.
PEST BUSTERS

IF THE CHRISTIAN RIGHT WERE SMART, THEY'D CONVERT ALL THOSE EX-GAY OPERATIONS TO LESBIAN-FRIENDLY **SPERM BANKS.** THEY'D HAVE US ALL SO BUSY ECSTATICALLY PUMPING **BREAST MILK**, WE'D NEVER NOTICE THEM TAKING OVER THE WHOLE FREAKING WORLD.

OH, PLEASE. IF I WAS AFTER THE MISS MIDDLE AMERICA TITLE, BECOMING A SINGLE LESBIAN MOTHER IS NOT THE WAY I'D GO ABOUT IT.
AND THAT'S ANOTHER THING! HOW ARE YOU GONNA DO THIS ALL BY YOURSELF?
JAVA JONES

WELL, I WOULDN'T MIND HAVING A PARTNER, BUT IT JUST HASN'T HAPPENED. AND I'M NOT GETTING ANY YOUNGER. BESIDES, MILLIONS OF WOMEN DO IT EVERY DAY. HOW DIFFICULT CAN IT BE?

THUMPITTA THUMPITTA
CRASH!
RAFFI! WHAT DID I TELL YOU ABOUT ROLLERBLADING ON THE STAIRS?!
RING!

NOT WITHOUT YOUR HELMET!
CLARICE! I GOT YOUR PAGE! WHAT'S WRONG?
YOUR GROWLING CHILD
HERMIONE LEECH

TONI! THANKS FOR CALLING! QUICK QUESTION. RAFFI AND BILLY WERE JUST USING THE BATHROOM TOGETHER, AND, UH... IN SHORT, I FORGET HOW WE DECIDED TO EXPLAIN THE WHOLE UNCIRCUMCISED DEAL. Y'KNOW, SO HE DOESN'T FEEL BAD ABOUT BEING DIFFERENT.
EQUALITY BEGINS AT HOME LOBBY DAY
FREEDOM TO MARRY
VISITORS TO STATEHOUSE SIGN IN →

YOU CALLED ME OUT OF A MEETING WITH THE GOVERNOR FOR THIS? JESUS, CLARICE!
BILLY'S GOT A FUNNY PE-NIS!
I DO NOT!
KLUNKA!
ACTUALLY, BABE, NEVER MIND. I'VE GOT IT UNDER CONTROL.

AH...THE DAY'S TOIL IS DONE, AND OUR WEARY LABORERS CAN RELAX IN THE RESTORATIVE CAMARADERIE OF THEIR FRIENDS, NEIGHBORS, AND FAMILY.

LET'S FACE IT. MOST OF US'LL CURL UP AND DIE AFTER A WEEK WITHOUT OUR DVD PLAYERS AND SONIC TOOTH FLOSSERS.
TO STOCKPILE KIDNEY BEANS AND VERSACE EXFOLIATING BODY WASH GEL.
WHERE ARE YOU GOING?

IN THE DRIVEWAY...
TONI? WE NEED TO TALK. EVER SINCE BILLY SPENT THE DAY WITH RAFFI, HE WON'T STOP ASKING WHERE HIS FORESKIN IS. EXACTLY WHAT WENT ON OVER HERE?

OH, ANN, I THINK CLARICE MAY HAVE GIVEN A LITTLE LECTURE ON CIRCUMCISION. I GUESS IT CAME UP WHEN THE BOYS NOTICED THEY LOOKED DIFFERENT.

WELL IN THE FUTURE, I'D APPRECIATE IT IF YOU WOULDN'T DISCUSS PRIVATE MATTERS WITH MY SON.
I'M SURE CLARICE WAS JUST TRYING TO...

IN FACT, I DON'T THINK THERE'S GOING TO BE A FUTURE. I'VE TRIED TO KEEP AN OPEN MIND ABOUT YOU TWO, BUT THIS JUST MAKES ME VERY UNCOMFORTABLE.
FINE. TAKE A NUMBER.
MARRIAGE IS A BASIC HUMAN RIGHT
SLAM

AROUND THE HEARTH...
HI, BABY. I'M STARVED. WHAT'S FOR SUPPER?
LOOKS LIKE CHILI. FOR THE NEXT COUPLE YEARS.
KIDNEY BEANS
NUKE-O-MATIC

...AND TO KEEP PEOPLE AWAY FROM OUR FOOD SUPPLY, WE'RE GONNA NEED THIS **STUN GUN**.
DAD? I THINK IT'S TIME TO REVISIT THE IDEA OF FINDING YOU SOME VOLUNTEER WORK.
Y2K MART
YOUR PANIC IS OUR PROFIT
KIDNEY

the Sensuous Bookshop
311
©1999 BY ALISON BECHDEL
ONE AFTERNOON AT MADWIMMIN BOOKS...
DID YOU FIND ABSOLUTELY EVERYTHING YOU'RE LOOKING FOR?
UH... YES. THANKS. I'M ALL SET.
SO DIANE, I'VE NEVER BEEN TO A VEGAN SEDER BEFORE. WHAT DO WE DO ABOUT THE SHANK BONE?
OPEN ME CAREFULLY

OH, WE JUST USE PART OF AN OLD TOY DINOSAUR SKELETON. BUT THE EGG-LESS MATZO BALLS ARE LIKE EATING LEAD SHOT.
Y'KNOW, IF YOU LIKE THIS BOOK, YOU'LL LOVE THE NEW EROTICA ANTHOLOGY, "HOT AND BUTTERED."
LOIS.
NCR
EMILY DICKINSON'S INTIMATE LETTERS

THEA, I'M JUST TRYING TO PROVIDE A SERVICE.
I LIVE TO SERVICE. I MEAN, TO SERVE.
I'LL FINISH THIS. WHY DON'T YOU GO TIDY UP THE BUMPER STICKER DISPLAY.

IN THE BACK...
AFTER I WATER THE PLANTS, SHOULD I FILL THE WEB ORDERS?
DON'T BOTHER. THERE AREN'T ANY. AND DO YOU KNOW WHY? BECAUSE IF YOU DO A SEARCH FOR OUR WEB SITE, AN AD FOR THE ONLINE BOOKSELLING BEHEMOTH medusa.com SHOWS UP ON THE PAGE.

IT MAGICALLY SAYS "BUY BOOKS ON MADWIMMIN BOOKS." CLICK THE LINK, AND YOU'RE IN THEIR CLUTCHES.

WILL THEY STICK AT **NOTHING?!**
THOSE ADS ARE PROGRAMMED TO SAY "BUY BOOKS ON" WHATEVER IT IS YOU'RE SEARCHING FOR. IT'S NOT, LIKE, INTENTIONAL.
YEAH, RIGHT. MY ONLY CONSOLATION IS, THEY'RE TROUNCING THE ONLINE SALES OF **BUNNS & NOODLE** AND **BOUNDERS, BOOKS & MUZAK**, TOO.
LATEST CASUALTIES: FULL CIRCLE BOOKS ALBUQUERQUE; RED & BLACK BOOKS, SEATTLE

... AND THEY'RE STILL NOT TURNING A PROFIT.
CUTTHROATS! THEY EVEN HAVE TO WIN AT LOSING.
DESPITE LOSSES, medusa.com STOCK UP 1000%

BYE, BABY. CALL ME WHEN YOU'RE DONE.
'KAY, LATER.
BUMPERSTICKERS
I'M POLLUTING THE
MEAT PEOPLE SUC
got bovine grow hormone?

WHOA! SOPHIE AND MRS. ROBINSON? THE KID'S GOOD!
LOIS, THAT'S HER MOTHER.

OH. WELL THEN, IS SHE AVAILABLE?
DEAR GOD, I HOPE NOT.

DON'T WORRY, JEZANNA. THIS ONLINE SHOPPING FAD WON'T LAST. HOW CAN BUYING A BOOK ON YOUR COMPUTER COMPARE WITH BROWSING THROUGH REAL BOOKS, THE HEFT OF AN ELEGANT VOLUME IN YOUR HAND...
... THE SATISFACTION OF KNOWING YOUR MONEY IS **SUSTAINING** COMMUNITY, NOT **LAYING WASTE** TO IT.
... AND LET'S NOT FORGET THE WARMTH OF HUMAN INTERACTION WITH SOMEONE WHO KNOWS EXACTLY WHAT YOU LIKE.
MILLIONS FOR MUMIA
March on Philly
APRIL 24
LESBIAN RIGHTS SUMMIT
D.C.
APR. 2

a just war?
or
just a war?

312

"ETHNIC CLEANSING" IS A TERRIBLE THING, BUT IT'S NOT THE SAME AS GENOCIDE. AND WHEN OFFICIALS TOSS THAT WORD AROUND FOR SPIN CONTROL, IT'S AN INSULT TO VICTIMS OF THE NAZIS, TO NATIVE AMERICANS, TO THE TUTSIS...

I THINK IT'S AN INSULT **NOT** TO CALL THIS GENOCIDE. AS A KID I ASKED MY GRANDPARENTS WHY THEY DIDN'T DO ANYTHING AFTER THEY FOUND OUT ABOUT THE HOLOCAUST. I'D BE A HYPOCRITE NOT TO SUPPORT GROUND TROOPS NOW!

dustup
©1999 BY ALISON BECHDEL
313
HI, SPANKY! UH... WHAT'RE YOU DOING?
OH. I DIDN'T THINK YOU'D MIND. YOUR MODEM'S SO MUCH FASTER THAN MINE. I WAS JUST LOOKING FOR SOME REAL INFORMATION TO COUNTER THIS REGURGITATED PENTAGON BRIEFING THAT PASSES FOR TV NEWS.
...COMING UP NEXT ON THE ABS EVENING NEWS, COOL COCKPIT VIDEOS OF THE CRISIS IN YUGOSLAVIA.

I'D RATHER YOU DIDN'T FOOL AROUND ON MY COMPUTER. UH...I JUST FINISHED ALL MY GRADING AND I HAVEN'T BACKED IT UP YET.
HEY, SYDNEY, D'YOU HAVE THAT GAME 'NANOSAUR?'
HI. I'M BOB DOLE, AND I SUFFER FROM E.D.,...

I DON'T HAVE ANY GAMES, MO. I REALLY WISH YOU WOULDN'T...
OH, NO? THEN WHAT'S IN THIS FOLDER? THE ONE SO CRYPTICALLY LABELED 'GAMES?' IS THAT WHERE YOU HIDE YOUR CLASSIFIED DOCUMENTS?
...ERECTILE DISINHIBITION. IN FACT, I HAVE A HARD ON RIGHT NOW.
SODA

DON'T OPEN THAT!
WHY NOT? WHAT'S IN HERE?
GINGKO INFUSED PARSLEY SODA

AAA!
OOPS.
KLUNK

MEANWHILE, IN ANOTHER TAX BRACKET...
YEAH, ANN WAS OVERREACTING ABOUT THE CIRCUMCISION DISCUSSION. IT'S NOT RIGHT TO KEEP THE BOYS APART JUST BECAUSE THE GROWN-UPS HAVE A DISAGREEMENT.
WELL, I THINK TONI FLEW OFF THE HANDLE A BIT HERSELF. SO RAFFI CAN STILL GO TO THE **STAR WARS** MOVIE WITH YOU SATURDAY?

OF COURSE! SO HOW'S THE "ENVIRONMENTAL JUSTICE" RACKET?
PRETTY GOOD. WE JUST TOOK ON A SUIT AGAINST A REAL DIRTBAG DEVELOPER. THIS GUY SOLD LAND TO THE CITY FOR LOW INCOME HOUSING THIRTY YEARS AGO, AND DIDN'T MENTION IT USED TO BE A PETROCHEMICAL DUMP.
NO KIDDING.
YEAH. AND NOT ONLY THAT, HIS LAWYERS CLAIM THE REASON THERE'S SO MUCH CANCER AMONG THE RESIDENTS IS BECAUSE THEY **SMOKE** MORE THAN AVERAGE! CAN YOU BELIEVE THOSE **MORAL IMBECILES?**

SOUNDS LIKE A PERFECTLY REASONABLE DEFENSE TO ME. THESE CANCER CLUSTERS ARE NOTORIOUSLY DIFFICULT TO TRACE TO AN UNDERLYING ENVIRONMENTAL CAUSE.
THANKS FOR THE VOTE OF CONFIDENCE. BILL. YOU SHOULD REPRESENT THIS GUY.

I ALREADY DO. AND ON SECOND THOUGHT, I'D RATHER GO ALONE WITH BILLY TO "EPISODE ONE." YOU KNOW. DO SOME FATHER-SON BONDING.

PERFECT! MAYBE YOU CAN LURE HIM OVER TO THE DARK SIDE OF THE FORCE WITH YOU!

boy trouble

314
MEEMA, LOOK!
OH MY GOD! CALL THE AMBULANCE! THAT'S THE WORST CASE OF FINGER-NAIL FUNGUS I'VE EVER SEEN!

IT'S NOT FUNGUS! IT'S POLISH, SEE? IT'S ALL SPARKLY!
OH, PHEW! WE WON'T HAVE TO AMPU-TATE! THAT'S REALLY COOL, RAF.

EMILY BROUGHT IT TO SCHOOL. I HAVE IT ON MY TOES TOO.
HI, BABE. DID YOU SEE OUR LITTLE FASHION PLATE?

YES, I DID. RAFFI, DID YOU TELL MEEMA WHAT HAPPENED?
NO.
OH. JOY.

WELL, UM, TAYLOR SAID ONLY GIRLS WEAR NAIL POLISH AND SO I, SO I SAID BUT I'M A BOY AND **I'M** WEARING NAIL POLISH, AND SO YOU'RE **WRONG**!
RAFFI, I'M PROUD OF YOU! THAT WAS A VERY SMART THING TO SAY!

AND THEN I KICKED HIM.

MEANWHILE...
AMAZING. YOU'D THINK THAT IN THE STAGGERING AMOUNT OF NEWS ANALYSIS THIS ISSUE HAS GENERATED, SOMEONE WOULD HAVE AT LEAST MENTIONED THE INTERESTING LITTLE COINCIDENCE THAT ALL THESE PISTOL-PACKIN' PUBESCENTS ARE MALE?
ALIENATED STUDENTS
USA DISMAY
LITTLETON MASSACRE
TEEN SHOOTERS
EPIDEMIC OF YOUTH VIOLENC

WHITE BOYS. CAN YOU IMAGINE IF IT WAS GIRLS, OR AFRICAN-AMERICAN KIDS WIPING OUT THEIR HOMEROOMS WITH TEC-9s? ALL THESE LAMENTS ABOUT OUR GENERIC "CHILDREN" WOULD GET AWFUL SPECIFIC AWFUL QUICK.
USA PATÉ
PREZ: "WE MUST TEACH OUR CHILDREN TO RESOLVE CONFLICTS WITH WORDS, NOT WEAPONS. ONCE THEY'RE ADULTS, THEY CAN USE CRUISE MISSILES."
Sale

WELL, MAYBE IT'S JUST THAT EVERYONE TAKES FOR GRANTED THAT BOYS ARE MORE PRONE TO VIOLENCE.
DUH! MALE VIOLENCE IS INVISIBLE. NO ONE WANTS TO LOOK AT IT AS A PROBLEM. THEY'D RATHER BLAME ANYTHING ELSE.
IT'S THE SUBURBAN ANOMIE
USA MELÉE
IT'S THE VIDEO GAMES
IT'S THE MUSIC
IT'S THE INTERNET
BRING BACK SCHOOL PRAYER

I MEAN, I'M SURE ALL THAT AGGRESSION CAME IN HANDY BACK IN THE PLEISTOCENE, BUT COME ON! LET'S EVOLVE A LITTLE, BOYS!
UH... RIGHT.
USA HURRAY
MADELINE ALBRIGHT TO MILOSEVIC: NEGOTIATE THIS, SLOBO.
MILANOS WITH ECHINACEA

MS. KISSLER THINKS PERHAPS HE'S NOT GETTING ENOUGH ROUGHHOUSING AT HOME. YOU KNOW, WHAT WITH HAVING TWO MOTHERS AND ALL.
OH REALLY? PERHAPS MS. KISSLER COULD USE A LITTLE ROUGHHOUSING HERSELF.

HAVING TROUBLE FINDING ROOM IN YOUR INSANE SCHEDULE FOR ALL THE ELEMENTS OF A FULL, BALANCED LIFE?

MULTITASK ALONG WITH GINGER!

WHILE KNOCKING OFF HER RESPONSIBILITIES AS A DUTIFUL DAUGHTER, A CARING PET OWNER, AND A CONSCIENTIOUS NEIGHBOR, SHE KEEPS UP WITH THE LATEST NEWS!

AND WHILE SIMULTANEOUSLY BREAKFASTING AND COMMUTING TO WORK, SHE DOES HER POLITICAL ACTIVISM!

TEACHING COLLEGE ENGLISH IS ALL-CONSUMING, BUT GINGER RENEWS HERSELF ON THE JOB WITH SPIRITUALLY CENTERING VISUALIZATION EXERCISES!

At home, she successfully juggles her obligations as a collective household member and her commitment to a nurturing diet of whole, unprocessed foods.

Many of us end up putting exercise and intimate time with friends on the back burner, but not Ginger!

While staying current in her field, our well-rounded gal checks one last task off the list!

idle hands
©1999 BY ALISON BECHDEL
316
AH, SUMMER VACATION! HAGGARD AND SPENT FROM THEIR STRESSFUL JOBS, SPARROW AND GINGER FINALLY GET SOME TIME OFF TO RECUPERATE.

THEIR HOUSE, THAT IS.
GOD, I HOPE THIS ISN'T LEAD PAINT. I DON'T HAVE ANY BRAIN CELLS TO SPARE.
SPEAKING OF ENVIRONMENTAL HAZARDS...
WAL-MART, AFTER BECOMING THE NATION'S SECOND LARGEST DRUG RETAILER...

HOW'S OUR FRIEND SYDNEY? HAS SHE DUMPED MO FOR THE CYBERSLUT YET?
OH, COME ON! YOU STILL THINK SYDNEY'S HAVING AN AFFAIR JUST BECAUSE...
MAGIC HAT
...BY PUTTING SCORES OF SMALLER STORES OUT OF BUSINESS...

JUST BECAUSE OF THOSE ONLINE CAPERS WITH LITTLE MISS "GOODTHING" I FOUND ON HER COMPUTER? WAKE UP, GINGER!
YEAH, WELL, YOU MAY BE RIGHT AFTER ALL. MO SAYS SYDNEY'S BEEN ACTING WEIRD LATELY, SECRETIVE.
...HAS ANNOUNCED IT WILL NOT BE CARRYING THE 'MORNING AFTER' EMERGENCY CONTRACEPTION PILL.

NOW DO YOU AGREE WE SHOULD WARN HER?
OH, SPARROW! WHAT WOULD WE SAY? "WE THINK YOUR GIRLFRIEND'S SCREWING AROUND ON YOU, BUT WE'RE NOT SURE, AND ANYWAY IT MIGHT ONLY BE VIRTUAL?"
WHEN ASKED IF THEY HAD ANY CONCERN ABOUT USING SHEER CORPORATE FORCE TO IMPOSE THEIR MORALITY ON WOMEN...

VIRTUAL SCHMIRTUAL. HOW LONG WILL THAT LAST? YOU KNOW WHAT LESBIANS ARE LIKE. THEY'LL CHAT ONLINE, THEY'LL PHONE, THEY'LL MEET, THEN SYDNEY'S OUTTA HERE.
WELL, MAYBE.
...BY LIMITING AVAILABLE HEALTH CARE OPTIONS, A WAL-MART SPOKESMAN HAD THIS TO SAY:

THAT EVENING, MO CONTINUES TO WONDER IF PERHAPS SYDNEY'S ATTENTION IS NOT UNDIVIDED.

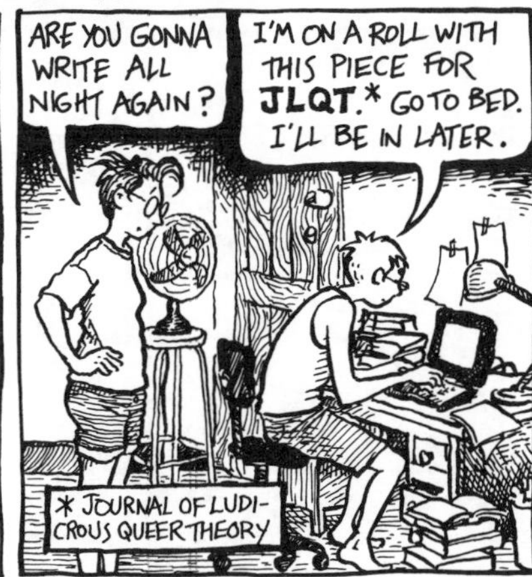

bewitched, bothered, & betrayed

317

MO'S HAVING TROUBLE FALLING ASLEEP WHILE SYDNEY'S STILL UP DOING GOD KNOWS WHAT ON HER COMPUTER.

A TIP O' THE NIB CATHY RESMER

WE HAVE A GENEROUS BENEFITS PACKAGE!
EAT ME! I'M GOOD FOR YOU!
SYDNEY'S ALREADY HAD A TASTE!

GAAH!

THREE O'CLOCK! HOW'M I SUPPOSED TO SLEEP WHEN SHE'S UP FUTZING AROUND?!

SYDNEY?

UH-HUH...

... BLACK SILK CAMISOLE WITH STRAPS THAT CROSS IN THE BACK... UH HUH ... YEAH...

WHO ARE YOU TALKING TO?
HEY, I GOTTA RUN. SOMEONE'S AT THE DOOR.

busted

318

MO HAS JUST DISCOVERED SYDNEY ENGAGED IN A DISCUSSION OF INTIMATE UNDERGARMENTS WITH AN AS-YET-UNIDENTIFIED THIRD PARTY IN THE HALL CLOSET AT 3 AM.

POPCORN? **POPCORN?!** ARE YOU **MAD?** HOW CAN I EAT POPCORN WITH MY **GUTS RIPPED OUT?**

OH, COME NOW. THERE'S NO NEED FOR MELODRAMA! I SAID I WAS SORRY!

NEXT DAY AT MADWIMMIN BOOKS, GINGER & SPARROW ARRIVE A BIT EARLY FOR THEIR LUNCHEON ENGAGEMENT WITH MO.

MEANWHILE, UPSTAIRS...

GoodThing: I love how you've decoupaged my thighs, Ms. Stewart. Now let me help you take off that handsome yet bulky cable-knit turtleneck.
CraftyGirl: Don't be so eager, my little scullion. Do I have to get out the macrame wrist restraints?
GoodThing: Yes, please! Tie me down on your 310 thread count sheets!

MO HAS BEEN CAUGHT IN A RATHER COMPROMISING POSITION WITH THE OLD COMPUTER.

ACTUALLY, IT WAS STUART WHO WAS SNOOPING.
STUART?! JESUS! IS THERE ANYONE LEFT WHO DOESN'T KNOW THE INTIMATE DETAILS OF MY FANTASY LIFE?

THAT DECOU-PAGE SCENE WAS HOT. YOU KNOW, IT RE-MINDS ME OF SOMETHING...
WELL, WE DIDN'T KNOW IT WAS YOU! THAT'S JUST IT! WE THOUGHT SYDNEY WAS HAVING AN AFFAIR WITH SOMEONE. WE WERE CONCERNED!
YOU JUST ASSUMED SYDNEY MUST BE FOOLING AROUND ON ME?

I DIDN'T WANT TO TELL YOU, BUT SPARROW WAS CONVINCED YOU'D THANK US.
GOT IT!
SO YOU THINK I'M A PATHETIC STOOGE, AND SYDNEY'S A DOU-BLE CROSSING WEASEL? IS THAT IT?

MO, WE JUST DIDN'T WANT TO SEE YOU GET HURT.
YOU DON'T EVEN KNOW SYDNEY! SHE'D NEVER BETRAY ME LIKE THAT!
FLIP!

CHECK IT OUT. THERE'S A STORY IN HERE ABOUT TWO CHICKS WITH A MARTHA STEWART THING.
WHAT'RE YOU DOING WITH THAT DISGUSTING RAG?
JUST READ IT.
VIAGRA®
LET THE DANCE BEGIN
PANTHOUSE
IMPLANT -O- RAMA
menu
A TIP O' THE NIB TO SEÑOR LORENZO SCHIMEL!

OH MY GOD! SHE'S SOLD OUR SEX LIFE TO "PANTHOUSE!"
VERBATIM!
PANTHOUSE

LATEST EXPLOITS

320

MO HAS JUST LEARNED THAT SYDNEY PUBLISHED A PARTICULARLY PRURIENT PORTION OF THEIR ONLINE INTERCOURSE IN "PANTHOUSE" MAGAZINE.

JESUS, SYDNEY! IT WAS WORD FOR WORD! YOU DIDN'T EVEN HAVE THE DECENCY TO **EDIT**!
UM... I WAS ON A TIGHT DEADLINE. I GUESS YOU'LL BE WANTING HALF THE CHECK, THEN.
MILLENIUM MARCH ON WASHINGTON HAWKS LGBT ~~COMMUNITY~~ MARKET TO HIGHEST BIDDER.

NOT THE FREAKING POINT! YOU TOOK SOMETHING MEANINGFUL AND GENUINE AND YOU **SOLD** IT! THOUSANDS OF DEPRAVED MEN AND PROBABLY **LOIS** ARE JACKING OFF TO IT **RIGHT NOW!**
BABE, I MADE A THOUSAND BUCKS AND SENT IT RIGHT TO ONE OF MY CREDIT CARDS!
VISIBILITY (FOR CORPORATE SPONSORS) A SOLID PLANK OF MARCH PLATFORM

BESIDES, I USED A PSEUDONYM!
I DON'T THINK I CAN HAVE THIS CONVERSATION RIGHT NOW. I NEED TO GO TALK TO SOMEONE WITHOUT A PERSONALITY DISORDER!
"THE BRAND-BUILDING OPPORTUNITIES ARE STAGGERING!" REPORTS MMOW FLACK.

BUT WHAT ABOUT DINNER? I'M COOKING **OSSO BUCO** OUT OF TEXTURIZED VEGETABLE PROTEIN, JUST THE WAY YOU...
SLAM!
...LIKE IT.
MARCH ORGANIZERS TO CRITICS: "HEY! VISUALIZE ABUNDANCE!"

LET'S JUST KEEP THE $3K I MADE ON THOSE PREVIOUS STORIES UNDER OUR HATS, SHALL WE?

A VISIT TO THE LOCAL ELEMENTARY SCHOOL STIRS UP FOND MEMORIES FOR CLARICE.

MEANWHILE, MO, STILL BRUISED FROM SYDNEY'S "PANTHOUSE" PERFIDY, TURNS FOR SUCCOR TO HER TRUSTY EX, HARRIET.

THE SITUATION IN SUBURBIA IS ESCALATING.

AND IN THE WAKE OF THE MOST RECENT ASSAULT, RAPPROCHEMENT BETWEEN MO AND SYDNEY APPEARS INCREASINGLY REMOTE.

BREAKFAST IN BED FOR A MONTH?
NO.
HOUR-LONG FULL BODY MASSAGE WITH SCENTED OIL?
NO.
ROMANTIC DINNER FOR TWO AT LA LENTILLE D'OR?
WOULD I HAVE TO GO WITH **YOU?**
TRAVEL

C'MON, MO. THROW ME A BONE.
SYDNEY, I'M AT WORK. CAN WE DO THIS LATER?
NAIAD PRESS
HITACHI
SCORPIO ADULT NOVELTIES

HEY, PROFESSOR. I HAVEN'T RECEIVED YOUR TEXTBOOK ORDER YET. I NEED IT BY FRIDAY IF YOU WANT BOOKS IN TIME FOR CLASSES.
GO AHEAD. TELL HER.
UH... ACTUALLY, JEZ, SINCE BUNNS & NOODLE TOOK OVER THE CAMPUS BOOKSTORE, MY DEPARTMENT HEAD'S PRESSURING US TO ORDER THROUGH THEM.
TRAVEL

AND YOU'RE GONNA LISTEN? OTHER PROFS ARE STANDING UP TO THEM. WHAT CAN THE UNIVERSITY DO? SEND OUT SOME D. LIT. CANDIDATE TO ROUGH YOU UP?
LOOK, AFTER I GET TENURE, I'LL FLOUT THE ADMINISTRATION ALL YOU WANT. BUT I CAN'T AFFORD TO ROCK THE BOAT JUST NOW.

HEY, SYD. CHECK OUT THE LATEST TECHNOLOGY. TRANSLUCENT JEWEL-TONE **PVC**.
GARISH, YET STRANGELY BEGUILING.
POLY-VINYL-CHLORIDE?
WHEN THEY MAKE BACKBONES OUT OF THAT STUFF, CALL ME.

I.D. fixe?
©1999 BY ALISON BECHDEL
323
YOUR MAIL.
BRIDE'S MAGAZINE?
SPLAP!

IS THERE SOMETHING YOU'D LIKE TO TELL ME, SPARROW? ASIDE FROM THE FACT THAT ORGANZA IS BACK?
OH MY GOD! I BET MY MOM DID THIS! EVER SINCE I CAME OUT TO HER ABOUT STUART, SHE THINKS IT MEANS I'M STRAIGHT. SHE CAN'T UNDERSTAND THAT I'M A **BISEXUAL LESBIAN!**
BRIDE'S
Cancun!
ORGANZA! IT'S BACK!

WELL, IT'S A NUANCE THAT CAN ELUDE THE BEST OF US.
LOOK, IN A PERFECT WORLD, I WOULDN'T HAVE TO CALL MYSELF ANYTHING. BUT FOR NOW, BI-DYKE WORKS FOR ME, OKAY?
HMO PHOBIC
NGUYEN'S BAGELS

I THINK I'M A BUTCH LESBIAN IN A STRAIGHT MAN'S BODY.
SOFT BUTCH. **MAY-**BE.
IT'S NOT AS SIMPLE FOR EVERYONE AS IT IS FOR YOU, GINGER! SOMETIMES PEOPLE CHANGE. IDENTITY IS SO MUCH MORE COMPLEX AND FLUID THAN THESE RIGID LITTLE CATEGORIES OF STRAIGHT, GAY, AND BI CAN POSSIBLY REFLECT.

YOU'RE A SWEETHEART, LOIS. SEE YA LATER.
'KAY, JERRY. HAVE FUN.

WHO WAS THAT? DON'T TELL ME YOU'RE SEEING A MAN TOO.
NO, JUST LENDING HIM A TIE. THOUGH HE IS KIND OF HOT.

HE REMINDS ME OF SOMEONE... WHATSERNAME... YOU KNOW, THAT BUFF BABE, YOUR MECHANIC?
GERALDINE, EXACTLY. ONLY NOW HE'S A BUFF TRANS GUY, AND HIS NAME'S JERRY.

ARE YOU SERIOUS? LIKE, WITH SURGERY? AND TESTOSTERONE? GOD, I JUST CAN'T UNDERSTAND THAT!
UH..."SOMETIMES PEOPLE CHANGE?" "IDENTITY IS COMPLEX AND FLUID?" ANY OF THAT RING A BELL?

CHANGING YOUR BODY TO CONFORM TO A RIGID, CONVENTIONAL GENDER IDENTITY IS JUST MORE BINARY THINKING! WHAT WAS WRONG WITH BEING A BUTCH DYKE?
HE DOESN'T FEEL LIKE A BUTCH DYKE. HE FEELS LIKE A GAY MAN.
SKIP FLUID. PRESS "LIQUEFY."

OH MY GOD! GERALDINE FROM RAINBOW AUTOMOTIVE?! I USED TO HAVE SUCH A THING FOR HER! I MEAN HIM... I MEAN.. WOW!
DON'T GET TOO EXCITED, STU. HE GOES MORE FOR THE STUDHORSE TYPE.
HMO PHOBIC

trite and true

OKAY, I CAN GET OUT OF DEBT, SPEND A YEAR DOING RE-SEARCH, ANOTHER YEAR IN BARCELONA OR PARIS WRITING MY BOOK, THE YEAR AFTER THAT TREKKING IN NEPAL, AND STILL HAVE CHANGE LEFT OVER TO BUY A DECENT COUCH.
TIKKA TIKKA TIK
...THE INDONESIAN ARMY HAS RECEIVED OVER A BILLION DOLLARS OF MILITARY AID FROM THE US...
324

SYDNEY, GIVE IT UP. YOU'RE NOT GONNA WIN A MACARTHUR GENIUS GRANT.
... INCLUDING SECRET TRAININGS FOR THE SPECIAL FORCES WHO DIRECTED ANTI-INDEPENDENCE MILITIAS IN THEIR SLAUGHTER OF TIMORESE CIVILIANS...

I KNOW YOU'RE THREAT-ENED BY MY HIGH LEVEL OF ACHIEVEMENT, MO, BUT THAT'S NO REASON TO BE PISSY.
RIGHT. WELL. YOU SET THE WORLD ON FIRE. I'M GOING OVER TO HARRIET'S.
... AFTER ADMITTING THAT HE'D LOST CONTROL OF HIS TROOPS, INDONESIA'S GENERAL WIRANTO DEMONSTRATED HIS EMOTION ABOUT LEAVING EAST TIMOR BY PUBLICLY CROONING "FEELINGS."
NOT MADE UP!

FOR A SCINTILLATING DIS-CUSSION OF HER LATEST ULTRASOUND? I THOUGHT SHE WAS BORING YOU SILLY WITH ALL THAT BABY TALK.
HEY, HARRIET'S TRITE OBSERVATIONS ABOUT THE MIRACLE OF A NEW LIFE BEAT LISTENING TO YOU ANY DAY OF THE WEEK.
...THE US COMMANDER-IN-CHIEF OF THE PACIFIC RESPONDED WITH A MOVING RENDITION OF "WIND BENEATH MY WINGS."
MADE UP.

OKAY! YOU'VE MILKED THIS SYDNEY-IN-THE-DOGHOUSE. THING JUST ABOUT LONG ENOUGH. WHEN ARE YOU GOING TO STOP BEING MAD?
RING
...SO I WAS THE ONE WITH ALL THE GLORY...

HELLO?
HUH-WO, AUNTIE! DERE'S A WIDDLE BITTY BABY HERE TO TALK TO YOU.
AND YOU WERE THE ONE WITH ALL THE STRAIN...

I'M SORRY. YOU HAVE THE WRONG NUMBER.
CLIK!
MONICA?!
VIRGINIA? NO, IT'S SYDNEY. HANG ON.

I THINK YOUR MOTHER HAS OFFICIALLY LOST IT.
MOM? WHAT'S WRONG?

ROSE HAD THE BABY! A PERFECT LITTLE GIRL! OH, MONICA! SHE LOOKS JUST LIKE YOU DID, ONLY MUCH PRETTIER!
OH MY GOD! REALLY?!
WHAT? WHAT HAPPENED?!

MY SISTER-IN-LAW HAD HER BABY! I'M AN AUNT! MY BROTHER'S A FATHER! MY MOTHER'S A GRANDMA! MY DAD'S A...
I THINK I CAN GENER-ALIZE FROM THERE.

OH MY GOD! SHE LOOKS LIKE ME! A NEW LIFE! TINY FINGERS AND TOES! IT'S A MIRACLE!
SHE LOOKS LIKE YOU? SNRK!
lunge
SIS? IT'S SCOTT. CAN YOU BELIEVE IT? LPGA, HERE WE COME! MAYBE SHE'LL EVEN BE A LESBIAN! THE BEST GOLFERS ALWAYS ARE, YOU KNOW.

325

YOU WENT TO THE PARK ALREADY? THAT WAS QUICK.
WE ONLY MADE IT TO THE END OF THE BLOCK. SHE'S HAVING A BAD DAY.
OOF! C'MON, PUP. YOU CAN DO IT.

JERRY LENT ME ONE OF HIS DIRTY UNIFORMS. WHAT DO YOU THINK? MAX AXLE, FRONT END EXPERT. I'M GONNA LIP-SYNCH TO "I'M YOUR VEHICLE, BABY."
GOD, THIS DRAG KING CRAZE IS SO RETROGRADE! MEN ARE DESTROYING THE PLANET! WHY COMPETE TO SEE WHO CAN MIMIC THEM MOST CONVINCINGLY?!
SEE OUR NEW SHOOTING SPREE SECTION FOR MORE NEWS

UH... BECAUSE I'M GOOD AT IT?
NASCAR
I DUNNO, LOIS. IT JUST SEEMS SO... SO MISOGYNIST. I COULD UNDERSTAND IF YOU WERE CRITIQUING MASCULINE STEREOTYPES INSTEAD OF GLORIFYING THEM, BUT...

ONE COULD ARGUE THAT DRAG IS THE ULTIMATE CRITIQUE OF GENDER STEREOTYPES, AND THUS INHERENTLY FEMINIST...
OH, PUT IT IN A TERM PAPER! LOOK, IT'S JUST A WAY OF EXPRESSING MY MASCULINE SIDE. MAYBE I AM GLORIFYING MASCULINITY. IS THAT SO TERRIBLE?
WOOOOOOO

HEY, WHO USED UP ALL MY ROSEMARY-CUCUMBER CONDITIONER? I NEED IT TO KEEP MY BEARD SILKY!

A REAL MACK-DADDY IS A GLORIOUS THING.
DUDE, JUST RUB A LITTLE CASTROL 30 WEIGHT INTO IT. WORKS FOR ME.
NASCAR

LABOR of LOVE
326
©1999 BY ALISON BECHDEL

REMEMBER, RAF. NO KICKING!
NOT EVEN THE BALL?
ZIP!
CARLOS, MAKE SURE HE USES HIS INHALER IF HE STARTS WHEEZING.

BYE, SWEETIE!
HAVE FUN DOING WHATEVER IT IS YOU GIRLS DO TOGETHER.

I WISH YOU WOULDN'T DISCUSS OUR SEX LIFE WITH HIM.
WHAT SEX LIFE?

OKAY, OKAY. LET'S NOT GET INTO A BIG DISCUSSION. THAT ALWAYS RUINS IT.
NO TALK. SUITS ME FINE.

SHORTLY...
The Distress

OH! IT'S GONNA SNOW TONIGHT! WE HAVE TO BRING IN THE GRILL AND LAWN CHAIRS!
SHHH... NO TALK.
AT HISTORIC DINNER, JERRY FALWELL'S SUPPORTERS AND GAY & LESBIAN CHRISTIANS AGREE TO DISAGREE

TONI, LOOK. IT'S JUST NOT WORKING FOR ME. I HAVE TO BE IN THE MOOD.
IF WE WAITED UNTIL WE WERE BOTH IN THE MOOD AND BOTH HAD TIME, WE'D BE DEAD. THAT'S WHY WE AGREED TO SCHEDULE IT!
EVANGELICALS SAY IT WAS DELICIOUS. GAYS CALL TURKEY TETRAZZINI "AN ABOMINATION."

ALL I CAN THINK ABOUT IS THOSE REPUBLICANS VOTING DOWN THE COMPREHENSIVE TEST BAN TREATY! IT'S LIKE THEY **WANT** US TO BURN UP IN A NUCLEAR ARMAGEDDON!

AND HOW 'BOUT THE POSSIBILITY THAT OUR NEXT PRESIDENT COULD BE A MAN WITH THE CULTURAL LITERACY OF A HEAD OF **ICEBERG LETTUCE**? DOESN'T **THAT** COOL YOUR ARDOR?
GET YOUR STORY STRAIGHT, CLARICE. IS IT THE ELECTION, NUCLEAR HOLOCAUST, OR THE LAWN FURNITURE?
GEORGE W: "ONCE I READ A BOOK BY JOHN LA CARE, ER... CARRIER? WHATEVER. MY CAMPAIGN BUDGET EXCEEDS THE G.N.P."

I BET YOU'D FOCUS PRETTY DAMN QUICK IF IT WAS **GINGER** LYING HERE INSTEAD OF **ME**.

UH... THAT'S COMPLETELY UNTRUE! COME BACK, I'M INTO IT NOW!
I'M SURE YOU'LL DO JUST FINE ON YOUR OWN. WHEN YOU'RE DONE, COME HELP ME MOVE THE GRILL.

ON A VISIT TO HER BROTHER, SISTER-IN-LAW, AND **NEW NIECE**, MO APPEARS TO BE COMPLETELY BESOTTED.

327

UH, BABE? THERE'S SOMETHING I'VE BEEN WANTING TO DISCUSS WITH YOU, AND NOW SEEMS LIKE THE RIGHT TIME. I... I'D LIKE TO EXPLORE POLYAMORY.
THAT'S NICE. LIKE THE MORMONS?
DKNY

NOT POLYGAMY. **POLYAMORY.** HAVING OPEN, NONPOSSESSIVE RELATIONSHIPS WITH MULTIPLE PARTNERS.
YOU'RE HAVING AN **AFFAIR!** IT'S THAT VEGAN GRAD ASSISTANT, ISN'T IT? THE ONE WHO MADE US ADOPT A MANATEE!

BESTSELLERS **90%** OFF
BUY **2** & WE'LL PAY **YOU**

I'M NOT HAVING AN AFFAIR. I'M JUST SAYING, WHY CLOSE OURSELVES OFF TO LIFE'S RICH PAGEANT? IF ONE LOVER IS GOOD, WOULDN'T TWO OR THREE BE BETTER?
JESUS, SYDNEY! YOU MAKE IT SOUND LIKE OPENING A **FRANCHISE!**
STAFF PICK
CORPORATE HQ PICK
THE U.S.A. ON $10 A DAY
DOW 36,000
EHH..

HEY! WHAT ARE WE DOING IN **BOUNDERS** ?!
LOOK, TAKE YOUR TIME! I UNDERSTAND IT CAN BE THREATENING TO LET GO OF THE **PATRIARCHAL** RELATIONSHIP MODEL.
REMAINDERED LITERARY FICTION $1.99/GROSS

...PARTICULARLY AT A TIME WHEN THE LESBIAN AND GAY POLITICAL ESTABLISHMENT IS EAGER TO SEND THE MESSAGE THAT WE'RE ALL MORE MONOGAMOUS THAN **COTTON MATHER**.*
THERE'S SOMETHING WRONG WITH THAT ARGUMENT, BUT I'M TOO NUMBED BY CORPORATE **MONOCULTURE** TO FIGURE IT OUT!
JANE AUSTEN HOLIDAY GIFT PAK! $49.99
EMMA The NOVELIZATION
cd!
TUNES TO DO NEEDLEWORK BY
PRIDE -N- PREJUDICE TEA COSY
ANH!
*OLD PURITAN DUDE

NOW IF YOU'LL EXCUSE ME, I HAVE TO GET THIS CHILD OUT OF HERE BEFORE SOMEONE SELLS HER A "PAT THE BUNNY" WORKOUT VIDEO.
WAAAAH!

Holiday on ICE
328
©1999 BY ALISON BECHDEL

'TIS THE SEASON! AT MO & SYDNEY'S...
MO, I DON'T HAVE TIME FOR THIS. I HAVE A HUNDRED PAPERS TO GRADE. I'M JUST GONNA BUY PRESENTS LIKE A NORMAL PERSON.
FINE. FEED THE CONSUMER CAPITALIST MACHINE. ANNIHILATE YOURSELF WITH DEBT.
Buy.com
MOTHRA STEWART LIVING
DO IT YOURSELF GIFTS
PIPE KLEENRS
ELMY'S

IF YOU REALLY CARED ABOUT FIGHTING CAPITALISM, YOU'D TRY POLYAMORY. MONOGAMY IS JUST A DEVICE TO CONSOLIDATE WEALTH BY CREATING LEGAL HEIRS.
MAKE YOUR OWN I.P.O.
QUICK 'N E-Z

DO WE HAVE AN ACETYLENE TORCH?
Things.com
MARTHA STEWART

AT MADWIMMIN BOOKS...
AND THE LAST BOOK ON MY LIST IS "LOVE MAKES A FAMILY," IN HARDCOVER.
YEP, RIGHT HERE. LET ME KNOW WHEN YOU'RE READY TO CHECK OUT, I'LL BE WORKING ON THE WINDOW DISPLAY.
HARRY POTTER & THE GARGANTUAN ROYALTY CHECK
HARRY POTTER

OH, I WON'T BE BUYING ANYTHING. I JUST WANTED TO SEE THE ACTUAL BOOKS BEFORE I ORDERED THEM FROM MEDUSA.COM. THANKS FOR YOUR HELP.
THUMB THUMB

AT SPARROW, STU, LOIS AND GINGER'S DIGS...
BLACK COHOSH TINCTURE.
CHECK.
CANDLES.
CHECK.
FLAX OIL.
CHECK.
KAVA KAVA ROOT.
CHECK.
SUMMONING THE DARK LORD?

JUST MAKING SURE WE'VE GOT THE NECESSITIES ON HAND IN CASE OF A Y2K MELTDOWN.

OH, GINGER! DON'T FORGET TO STOCK UP ON DOG FOOD!
UM... RIGHT.

AND AT MIDTOWN MIDWIFERY SERVICES...
OH, JUST A SLIGHT SNOWBOARDING MISHAP. IT'S NOTHING. HOW ARE **YOU** FEELING?
NOT SO GREAT, ACTUALLY. I'VE HAD A SPLITTING HEADACHE ALL DAY.
IDITAROD
THE PREGNANT GUIDE TO ULTIMATE LESBIANISM

HMM. REALLY.
MIRIAM? IS EVERYTHING OKAY?

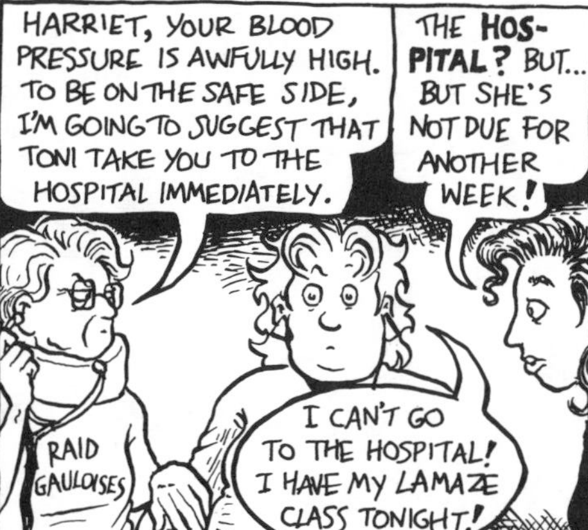
HARRIET, YOUR BLOOD PRESSURE IS AWFULLY HIGH. TO BE ON THE SAFE SIDE, I'M GOING TO SUGGEST THAT TONI TAKE YOU TO THE HOSPITAL IMMEDIATELY.
THE **HOSPITAL?** BUT... BUT SHE'S NOT DUE FOR ANOTHER WEEK!
I CAN'T GO TO THE HOSPITAL! I HAVE MY LAMAZE CLASS TONIGHT!
RAID GAULOISES

DyKes
Address http://www
click
this
©1999 by
Alison Bechdel

SORRY, READERS. THIS WEEK'S EPISODE HAS BEEN CANCELLED WHILE OUR STAFF SCRAMBLES BELATEDLY FOR A CRUMB OF THE e-PIE.
329

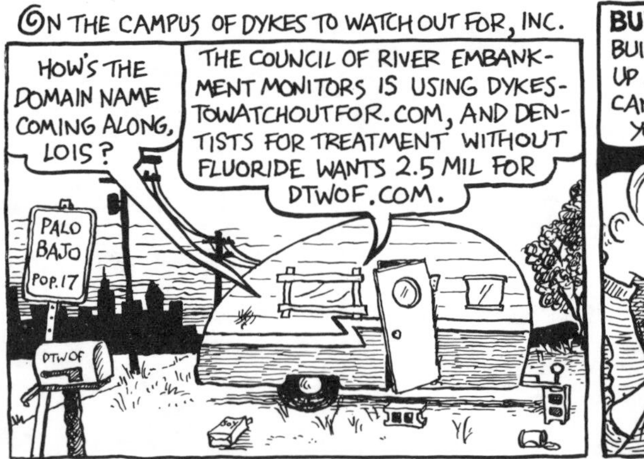
ON THE CAMPUS OF DYKES TO WATCH OUT FOR, INC.
HOW'S THE DOMAIN NAME COMING ALONG, LOIS?
THE COUNCIL OF RIVER EMBANKMENT MONITORS IS USING DYKESTOWATCHOUTFOR.COM, AND DENTISTS FOR TREATMENT WITHOUT FLUORIDE WANTS 2.5 MIL FOR DTWOF.COM.
PALO BAJO POP. 17
DTWOF

BUY IT! WE'VE GOTTA BUILD BRAND! IF WE END UP AS A DOT.NET, YOU CAN KISS RETIRING ON YOUR STOCK OPTIONS SAYONARA!

UH...BUY IT WITH WHAT?
PUT IT ON YOUR CREDIT CARD. I'LL PAY YOU BACK AFTER THE IPO.
HTML FOR NIT-WITS

JEZANNA, I DON'T KNOW ABOUT GOING PUBLIC. I THINK WE MAY HAVE LOST OUR WINDOW.
TONI? YOUR MOM CALLED. SHE SAYS ALL IS FORGIVEN, SHE'S JOINING PFLAG, AND SHE WANTS 100 SHARES.
JÉSUCRISTO.

WHAT DO YOU MEAN, LOST OUR WINDOW?
JUST ADDING DOT.COM TO YOUR NAME DOESN'T DO IT ANY MORE. WE NEED SOMETHING ELSE. SOMETHING WE CAN, LIKE, SELL.

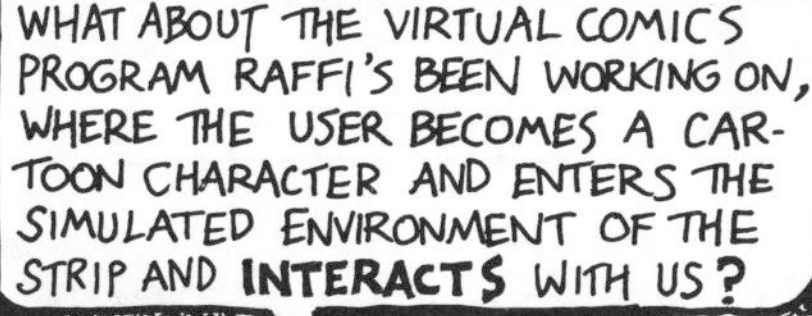
WHAT ABOUT THE VIRTUAL COMICS PROGRAM RAFFI'S BEEN WORKING ON, WHERE THE USER BECOMES A CAR-TOON CHARACTER AND ENTERS THE SIMULATED ENVIRONMENT OF THE STRIP AND INTERACTS WITH US?

CHECK IT OUT.

WE ALL LOOK LIKE POKÉMONS.
I'M WORK-ING ON IT. THIS IS JUST THE BETA.

THINK OF THE POSSIBILI-TIES! PEOPLE COULD MEET MO FOR BRUNCH! SPOT CARLOS ON THE BENCH PRESS! HAVE SEX WITH LOIS!
WHO TH'HELL WOULD PAY FOR THAT?
I'VE GOT A PLAN TO MONETIZE THE SITE, JEZ. SAY A READER LIKES THE SWEATER I'M WEARING. THEY CLICK ON IT...
VISA

...AND BINGO! PAPAYAREPUB-LIC.COM IS DOWNLOADING THEIR CREDIT CARD NUMBER!
SELLING PEOPLE MORE USELESS SHIT! I LIKE IT! BUT WE COULD SAVE OURSELVES A LOT OF TROUBLE BY GOING DIR-ECTLY TO SATAN.COM AND CASHING IN OUR SOULS!

HMM. INTERESTING, MO. THAT MIGHT BE A GOOD OPTION IF WE'RE UN-ABLE TO ATTRACT VENTURE CAPITAL.
WHAT HAPPENS IF I CLICK ON THE MO POKÉMON?

CLICK HER SHIRT AND YOU GO TO KMART.COM. CLICK HER HEAD AND SHE IMPLODES FROM THE TENSION BETWEEN HER CORE BELIEFS AND THE THINGS SHE HAS TO DO FOR THIS JOB.
COOL.
SPLORCH

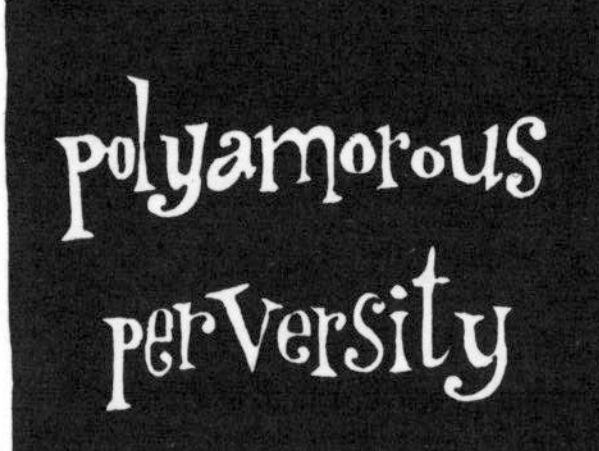

MO'S HOLIDAY CRAFTS PROJECT APPEARS TO HAVE BEEN DERAILED.

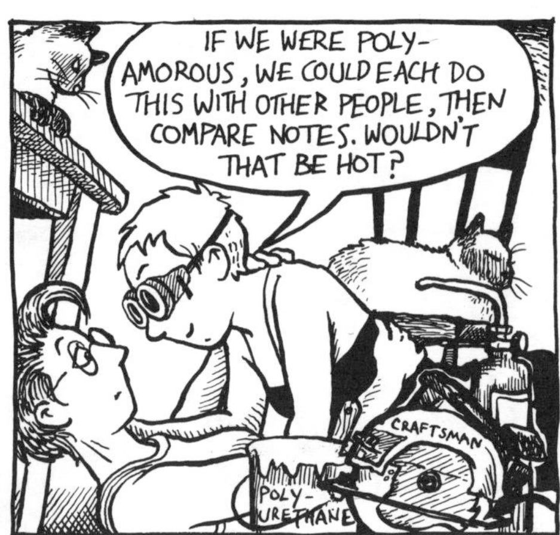

ACTUALLY, MO, I'VE BEEN MEANING TO TALK TO YOU ABOUT HOW INVOLVED YOU'VE GOTTEN WITH HARRIET'S PREGNANCY.
... MISGUIDED 'SIXTIES LEFTOVERS WHO WOULDN'T KNOW A TARIFF FROM A STICK OF DEODORANT...

INVOLVED? SHE'S MY BEST FRIEND!
SHE'S ALSO YOUR EX.
HOSPITAL PARKING
IF YOU WANT TO IMPROVE LABOR AND ENVIRONMENTAL STANDARDS IN DEVELOPING COUNTRIES, THE ANSWER IS FEWER RESTRICTIONS ON TRADE, NOT MORE.

YOU'RE JEALOUS OF HARRIET? GOD! Y'KNOW, YOU COULDN'T **HANDLE** POLYAMORY!
PARKING $3 IN ADVANCE
CHOMSKY
NEOLIBERALISM & GLOBAL ORDER
NO WTO
WHY? BECAUSE I GET PAID A LARGE SALARY BY THE GLOBAL MEDIA CONGLOMERATE THAT OWNS THIS STATION TO TELL YOU SO, **THAT'S** WHY.

SOON...
MO! LOOK! INSTANT HARRIET JUNIOR!
OH MY GOD! IS HARRIET OKAY?
SHE'S FINE. STILL DRIFTING IN AND OUT FROM THE ANESTHESIA. EVERY ONCE IN A WHILE SHE WAKES UP AND ASKS IF THE BABY'S ALL RIGHT. SHE ASKED FOR YOU TOO, MO.
MOAB

WOW, REALLY? SHE'S BEEN ASKING FOR ME?
HOW VERY TOUCHING.
WELL, TO PUT IT IN PERSPECTIVE, SHE'S ALSO BEEN ASKING FOR OPRAH.
I DO NOT **LIKE** GREEN EGGS AND HAM.

LUNCH MAKES A FAMILY
©1999 BY ALISON BECHDEL

331
GIVE HER TO ME, MO.
EHHH!
TONI, CAN YOU PUT THIS HERBAL WRAP BACK IN THE MICROWAVE A MINUTE?
RINGG!
CARLOS, WHERE'S MY FRIED EGG SANDWICH?
KEEP YOUR SHIRT ON.
VERMONT SUPREME COURT MAKES LAND-MARK DECISION

PESKY SINGLE MOTHERS. YOU'RE RUNNING THIS GREAT NATION INTO THE GROUND.
NOW FEED IT TO ME.

HARRIET, LET'S MOVE TO VER-MONT. I COULD MAKE A QUASI-HONEST WOMAN OF YOU.
COVER ME AND ISABEL WITH YOUR HEALTH PLAN, AND WE'LL FOLLOW YOU ANYWHERE.
LESBIAN AND GAY COUPLES DESERVE SAME BENEFITS AS NORMAL MAR-RIED PEOPLE

MO, IT'S YOUR GIRL-FRIEND.
THERE GOES THE HONEYMOON IN STOWE.

I SAID NO MAYO.
NO, I'M GONNA EAT HERE.... SYDNEY, YOU'LL BE FINE! BOIL SOME RAMEN OR SOMETHING!

MEANWHILE...
HELLO, BABY. SORRY I WAS AT WORK SO LONG. HOW'S MY SWEET GIRL?

SHE HARDLY GOT OFF HER BED ALL DAY.
GOD, SPARROW. I DON'T KNOW HOW TO MAKE THIS DECISION. SHE'S SO HAPPY TO SEE ME, BUT SHE CAN BARELY MOVE, AND SHE'S NOT EATING.
The Nation

ACTUALLY, SHE HAD A FEW BITES OF STEAK EARLIER. I BOUGHT ONE AND COOKED IT FOR HER. THE REST IS ON THE TOP SHELF OF THE FRIDGE IF YOU WANT TO GIVE HER MORE.

YOU COOKED A **STEAK?** IS THIS THE SAME WOMAN WHO ONCE TRIED TO CONVINCE ME DOGS COULD LIVE ON RICE AND BREWER'S YEAST BECAUSE SHE DIDN'T WANT **MEAT** IN THE HOUSE?

THAT'S DEVOTION, DIGGER.
LOOK, JUST DON'T TELL STUART I WAS SEARING FLESH IN HIS CALPHALON SAUTÉ PAN. HE'S EVEN MORE OF A PURIST THAN I AM.

HEY, I FINISHED OFF THAT SEITAN ON THE TOP SHELF OF THE FRIDGE. **DELICIOUS!** WHAT WAS IT MARINATED IN?

CLARICE HAS RUN INTO HER ~~NEMESIS~~ NEIGHBOR BILL AT THE LOCAL PARK WHERE THEIR RESPECTIVE CHILDREN ARE DISPORTING THEMSELVES.

OH, I GET IT. KINDA LIKE SAME-SEX MARRIAGE.
VERY FUNNY.

LOOK, I THINK YOU PEOPLE SHOULD HAVE THE SAME RIGHTS AS EVERYONE ELSE, BUT TWO MEN OR TWO WOMEN GETTING MARRIED IS JUST SILLY.

HUH. I GUESS YOU MISSED THAT DAY IN LAW SCHOOL WHEN THEY COVERED 'SEPARATE BUT EQUAL' BEING UNCONSTITUTIONAL.
HEY, HEY HEY!

RAFFI!
WHAT'S THE PROB-LEM HERE, GUYS?

I CAN TOO MARRY STONE COLD STEVE AUSTIN WHEN I GROW UP!
CLARICE, WHAT ARE YOU TEACH-ING THIS KID?

YOU CAN NOT, 'CAUSE I'M GONNA MARRY HIM, AND WE'RE GONNA KICK YOUR BUTT!
HISTORY UNFOLDING, BILL. YOU CAN WHINE AND DRAG YOUR FEET, BUT IT'S GONNA HAPPEN.

Village IDIOT
333
© 2000 BY ALISON BECHDEL

MO, WHAT ARE YOU **DOING?!** THE DEAN'S RECEPTION IS AT EIGHT! I'M JUST GONNA CHANGE MY CLOTHES, THEN WE HAVE TO LEAVE!
I DON'T FEEL SO GOOD, SYDNEY.
A TIP O' THE NIB TO WILL MARQUESS!
LOOK, I KNOW YOU HATE THESE THINGS, BUT I HARDLY EVER ASK YOU TO COME, AND THIS ONE'S IMPORTANT!
I THINK IT'S THE FLU. GO WITHOUT ME. YOU'LL BE FINE.

GOD, THIS FOURTH YEAR SCRUTINY IS KILLING ME. I WAS HOPING YOU COULD HELP ME SCORE SOME POINTS WITH THE DEAN TONIGHT.
HOW WOULD YOUR LESBO GIRLFRIEND POSSIBLY SCORE YOU POINTS?
ECO-BLOW
POLY-AMORY & YOU

BECAUSE MY PRESSED, STARCHED, LATIN PUN-SPEWING ARCHRIVAL **BETSY GILHOOLY** WILL BE THERE WITH **HER** GIRLFRIEND.
OH, RIGHT. THE ONE YOU'RE COMPETING WITH FOR TENURE.

AND TO TOP IT OFF, NOW THE GIRLFRIEND'S PREGNANT. THE DEAN'S VERY BIG ON CHILDREN. EVEN BIOENGINEERED ONES.
RING
HELLO?
MO, I THINK I HAVE THE FLU OR SOMETHING. I CAN'T GET OFF THE COUCH. CAN YOU COME OVER AND HELP WITH ISABEL?
SWINGATRONIC

OKAY, HARRIET. I'LL BE RIGHT THERE.
IF YOU'RE TOO SICK TO COME TO THE RECEPTION, YOU'RE TOO SICK TO GO PLAY HOUSE!
POINK!

HARRIET, MO'S A MESS. YOU'LL HAVE TO FIND ANOTHER NANNY. ... OH, REALLY?... EVERYONE? YOU DON'T SAY...
PC COMPACT FLUORESCENT BULB.

LATER THAT EVENING...
WHAT A NICE WAY TO END THE WORKDAY THESE COLLEGIAL GATHERINGS ARE, DEAN. OR AS I ALWAYS SAY, SIC TRANSIT GLORIA TUESDAY! AH HA HA HA HA!
QUITE.

MS. KRUKOWSKI! WHO'S THIS LITTLE CHERUB! I DIDN'T KNOW YOU WERE A PARENT!
WELL, DEAN, TECHNICALLY I'M JUST HELPING OUT A SICK FRIEND, BUT YOU KNOW WHAT THEY SAY- IT TAKES A VILLAGE TO RAISE A CHILD.

OLD DOG NEW TRICKS
©2000 BY ALISON BECHDEL

334
AAAH!

GOD, LOIS! I WISH YOU'D STICK TO ONE DRAG PERSONA.
COOL. YOU REALLY THOUGHT I WAS SOME SKEEVY GUY!
BIRCH BARK
TAMPONS WITH DIOXIN

I KNEW IT WAS YOU, BUT THAT SHIRT TRIGGERED A FLASH-BACK TO MY JUN-IOR PROM.
DAMN. MAYBE BIGGER SIDEBURNS?
DING DONG
1000 SHEETS
HEMPONS

WHAT'S HAPPENIN', PRETTY LADY?

HI, LOIS. CUTE SHIRT. I'M HERE TO SEE DIGGER.
SNICK

GINGER! THE VET'S HERE!
TIME FOR YOUR CHECKUP, BUMBLEPUPPY.
A TIP O' THE NIB TO LASKY, KIRA & WALTER!

MEANWHILE, IN SUBURBIA...
...OH, AND THIS AFTERNOON I FINALLY CONVINCED ANN NEXT DOOR TO HAVE SOME OF US FROM FREEDOM TO MARRY COME SPEAK TO HER **ROTARY CLUB** CHAPTER.
UH HUH.
FANNING THE ASHES

CLARICE, IF YOU WON'T STOP READING THAT BOOK LONG ENOUGH TO LISTEN TO ME, HOW'S IT SUPPOSED TO HELP OUR RELATIONSHIP?
HAULING the ASHES

WAIT, I'M JUST CHECKING TO SEE IF THE WORDS "ROTARY CLUB" ARE LISTED IN THE SECTION ON "EXPANDING YOUR EROTIC VOCABULARY."
HOW TO AVOID SEXUAL BOREDOM IN YOUR LONG-TERM RELATIONSHIP

BACK AT GINGER'S HOUSE...
HOW IS SHE?
SHE'S WEAK, BUT CLEARLY SHE'S STILL TAKING COMFORT IN EATING AND GETTING PETTED. YOU'LL HAVE TO DETERMINE WHEN THE DISCOMFORT STARTS TO OUTWEIGH THE PLEASURE. WHEN IT'S TIME, WE CAN DO IT RIGHT HERE.

BARAR-ARAR!!
BETTER THAN I THOUGHT.
THANKS, DIGGER. I'LL DEFINITELY KEEP THE MUTTON-CHOPS.

A FINE MESS
335
©2000 BY ALISON BECHDEL

THUD!
CRASH!
MADWIMMIN BOOKS
WE'RE EXPANDING CAFÉ OPENING SOON!
Open
café

...AND I WORKED OUT A DEAL WITH THE WOMEN WHO RUN THE CAFÉ NEXT DOOR, AND WE'RE CONNECTING OUR SPACES.
HUH. SO NOW PEOPLE CAN GET COFFEE STAINS AND CRUMBS ALL OVER YOUR BOOKS INSTEAD OF THE ONES AT BUNNS & NOODLE.
STRANGE SISTERS

Chunk!
EXACTLY. AND IN A COZIER ATMOSPHERE.

HEY, SOPH. HOW WAS SCHOOL?
THE USUAL CZARIST REGIME. OUR GAY/STRAIGHT ALLIANCE IS TRYING TO GET A BUS TO GO TO THE MARCH, AND IT'S LIKE WE SUGGESTED NEUTERING THE FOOTBALL TEAM.

WHAT MARCH?
THE MILLENNIUM MARCH? THE LESBIAN/GAY/BI/TRANS MARCH ON WASHINGTON? AREN'T YOU GOING?

OH, ABSOLUTELY! I'VE ALREADY GOT MY OFFICIAL DISCOUNT CARD, AND MY TICKET TO THE GARTH BROOKS CONCERT! AND I CAN'T WAIT TO SHOP AT THE GAY-FRIENDLY VENDOR BOOTHS! I'M FEELING SO EMPOWERED!
Y'KNOW, YOU THINK YOU'RE SUCH A BIG RADICAL, BUT YOU'RE REALLY JUST A WHINY ELITIST.
THUD!

HEY, THE BIGWIG MARCH ORGAN-IZERS ARE THE ELITISTS! THEY'RE THE ONES WHO DECIDED TO STAGE THIS DAMN THING WITH-OUT CONSULTING THE REST OF THE COMMUNITY.
MO, I'M SORRY THE GOOD OLD DAYS ARE GONE, WHEN EVERYONE SAT AROUND PROCESSING FOR YEARS BEFORE PUTTING UP A FLIER. BUT DON'T TRY AND RUIN THIS FOR ME!

I'M EXCITED ABOUT THIS MARCH AND I'M GOING!
WHAT MARCH?
CRASH
OFFICE

THAT EVENING...
SYDNEY! I THOUGHT YOU WERE GONNA CLEAN THE KITCHEN!
SORRY, BABE. I'VE BEEN WORKING ON THIS LECTURE.
PRETZO RODS
Rice Milk

WELL HOW AM I SUPPOSED TO COOK?!
OH, DON'T BOTHER. I'M NOT HUNGRY.
NUT TER
RICE MILK

HOOP DREAMS
PART 1

WHEW! THE LADY PORCUPINES ARE UP BY ONE AT THE HALFTIME BUZZER! TUNE IN NEXT TIME AS THE TECHNICAL FOULS CONTINUE!

WE LAST LEFT OUR SPORADIC SPORTSFANS AT HALF-TIME.

PLAY APPEARS TO HAVE RESUMED.

AND LOIS IS LOBBYING TOO...

SO JERRY, UH...D'YOU HAVE A BOYFRIEND YET?
NAH. LISTEN, I WANT TO GET BACK TO THE GAME, BUT COME BY THE GARAGE SOMETIME. IT'S BEEN TOO LONG. YOU MUST BE OVER-DUE FOR AN OIL CHANGE.
FWEET!

GINGER AND CLARICE FLIRT WITH A POSSIBILITY...
Y'KNOW, THERE'S A PICKUP GAME AT THE 'Y' WEDNESDAY NIGHTS. WE SHOULD GO SOMETIME.
THAT SOUNDS REALLY FUN. I HAVEN'T TOUCHED A BALL IN YEARS.

AND ACROSS THE BLEACHERS...
THE GLORIA? THE LEGEN-DARY GLORIA OF YOUR SEXUAL FANTASIES? SHOW HER TO ME!
WHERE'S CLARICE? HAS SHE BEEN GONE ALL THIS TIME?

HERE COMES LOIS. I GUESS I SHOULD GET BACK TO MY SEAT.
IT WAS, UM... REALLY NICE TALKING TO YOU.

OH, MAN. I'M IN TROUBLE. HAVE YOU EVER TOTALLY WANTED SOMEONE WHO WAS JUST, LIKE, WRONG?
WHAT?

LATER, AFTER THE LADY PORCUPINES SUFFER AN IGNOMINIOUS SHELLACKING...
WHAT A GREAT GAME!
WASN'T IT THRILLING?

flow state
DANG.
DISH GREEN
BIODEGRADABLE PHOSPHATE-FREE, WITH HEALING MAGNETS!
$3.99

WOW, THIS IS GREAT, DAD. THANKS... HEY, I BETTER GET STARTED. YEAH, OKAY. SAY HI TO, UH... JENNIFER.
The New York Times
GRIDLOCK STALLS SENATE
TRAFFIC CONGESTION WORSENS
Sunday Styles

THE SINK'S CLOGGED AGAIN.
DID YOU FOLLOW THAT? MY FATHER WAS JUST AT A RHETORIC CONFERENCE AND RAN INTO AN OLD FRIEND WHO EDITS **THEORETICAL CRITIQUES OF CRITICAL THEORY**! DAD TOLD HIM ABOUT MY WORK AND HE SAID HE'D STRONGLY CONSIDER A SUBMISSION BY ME!
BIP

THEORETICAL CRITIQUES OF CRITICAL THEORY?

I KNOW! WHAT A FEATHER IN MY CAP **THAT** WOULD BE! BETSY GILHOOLY WILL DROOL IF I GET PUBLISHED THERE! THE DEADLINE'S IN A WEEK, THOUGH, SO I HAVE TO CRANK.

GOODY. I WAS GETTING TIRED OF LIVING WITH A DRIVEN WORKAHOLIC. AN OBSESSED LUNATIC WILL BE A NICE CHANGE OF PACE.
I'VE BEEN WORKING ON AN IDEA ABOUT **POLYAMORY** AS A CRITICAL STRATEGY, AS A WAY OF EXPLORING A TEXT WITHOUT COMMITMENT TO A PARTICULAR METHODOLOGY. I JUST NEED TO FLESH IT OUT A BIT.

JUST REMEMBER WE'RE GOING TO CLARICE AND TONI'S FOR DINNER SATURDAY.
BABE, I'LL NEED TO WRITE ALL WEEKEND. BESIDES, I LIKE CLARICE AND TONI, BUT CHATTING ABOUT FIRST GRADE AND SAME-SEX MARRIAGE IS NOT MY IDEA OF STIMULATING DISCOURSE.

YEAH, WELL. I DOUBT THEY'D FIND 'POLYAMORY AS A CRITICAL STRATEGY' ALL THAT TITILLATING EITHER. LISTEN, THEY'RE MY FRIENDS. I WANT US TO SPEND TIME TOGETHER.
INVITE THEM HERE! THEN AFTER DINNER I COULD GO BACK TO WORK!
MONEY & BIZNESS
IS GROWTH SLOWING?

INVITE THEM **HERE?**
WHY NOT?

SYDNEY, THIS PLACE IS FILTHY! YOU HAVEN'T LIFTED A FINGER AROUND HERE ALL SEMESTER, AND I CAN'T DO EVERYTHING MYSELF!
YOU KNOW WHAT YOUR PROBLEM IS? YOU FEAR DISORDER. YOU HAVE THIS CALVINISTIC, PROTESTANT WORK ETHIC, ANAL-RETENTIVE THING GOING ON. WHEREAS I DON'T NEED THINGS TO BE TIDY. I CAN TOLERATE INDETERMINACY.

THIS IS NOT INDETERMINACY! THIS IS A SALMONELLA COLONY!

AND DON'T GIVE ME THAT WORK ETHIC THING! **YOU'RE** THE MOST WORK-OBSESSED PERSON I'VE EVER MET! YOUR CAREER HAS TAKEN OVER BOTH OUR LIVES! YOU CAN'T COMMIT TO A SIMPLE DINNER WITH FRIENDS...

WHOA! YOU COULD KNIT A SOCK OUT OF THAT ONE. YOU REALLY SHOULD BRUSH THOSE CATS ONCE IN A WHILE.

KAACK!

HAIR-BALL

DING DONG!
DID YOU KNOW A ANA... ANA... ANDACONDA IS SO BIG IT CAN EAT ALLIGATORS?
MY FIRST BOOK O' SNAKES

RAFFI! THAT'S CARLOS TO PICK YOU UP. DO YOU HAVE EVERYTHING YOU NEED IN HERE?
NO! I HAVE TO GET MONTY!
STALEMATE

DON'T GET TOO WRAPPED UP IN THAT. WE HAVE A DATE.
I KNOW, I KNOW. IT'S IN MY PLANNER UNDER 'CONJUGAL OBLIGATIONS.'
...AND NOW BACK TO **FARCE; THE NATION.**

HEY, MAMITA!
WHAT ARE YOU WEARING?!

NICE, HUH? MAYBE I'LL PASS FOR A PROFESSIONAL WITH SOME OF THE MORE ATTRACTIVE DADS DOWN AT THE PARK.
A PROFESSIONAL **WHAT.**

HEY, I PLAYED INTRAMURALS IN HIGH SCHOOL, DOÑITA.
INTRAMURAL BADMINTON.

WHATEVER. SO HOW ARE THINGS IN MONOGAMYVILLE? VIBRATOR ALL PLUGGED IN AND READY TO GO?
PLUG THIS IN, PELÉ.

OW! I'M JUST TRYING TO SHOW AN INTEREST IN YOUR CUSTOMS!
CARLOS, A WORD OF ADVICE. IF YOU REALLY WANT PEOPLE TO THINK YOU'RE A PRO, DON'T GO NEAR A SOCCER BALL.

YOU'RE SO CONGENIAL, CLARICE. NO WONDER TONI FANTASIZES ABOUT GLORIA WHEN YOU TWO GO AT IT.
WHAT?

G-L-O-R-I-AAY!
GLORIA? YOU'RE STILL THINKING ABOUT GLORIA?

NICE, CARLOS.
WHAT? HOW WAS I SUPPOSED TO KNOW? I THOUGHT LESBIANS TOLD EACH OTHER EVERYTHING!

GLORIA? BUT...BUT SHE MOVED TO ALBUQUERQUE FOUR YEARS AGO!
WELL, SHE'S BACK NOW. ¡RAFAEL! ¡MI GUANDULITO!* ARE YOU READY?
* MY LITTLE PIGEON PEA

AND OVER AT SPARROW, STUART, LOIS & GINGER'S DOMICILE...

EVEN WITH WOMEN? SO THEY WERE BETTER.
WILL YOU COME HERE?

I DON'T KNOW. I DON'T FEEL LIKE IT NOW.
STUART, I'M GETTING REALLY TIRED OF THIS.

I KNEW YOU WOULD EVENTUALLY.

A BIT LATER...

LOOK, I WANT TO BE WITH YOU! WHY CAN'T YOU SEE THAT? ALL THIS SEXUAL AND EMOTIONAL INSECURITY MAKES ME WONDER IF MAYBE YOUR SECOND CHAKRA ISN'T BLOCKED.
DO YOU THINK?

I DO FEEL SORT OF SLUGGISH, LIKE THERE'S THIS OBSTRUCTION SOMEWHERE INSIDE ME.
THESE USUALLY DO THE TRICK.
REAL ESTATE SALES STAGNANT
grape nuts
The SUNDAY DISTRESS
COLD FRONT STALLS OVER REGION

IT'S YOUR CHAKRAS. YOUR KUNDALINI ISN'T FLOWING.
UH... SHOULD I LEAVE?
ARF!

KUNDALINI IS THE DIVINE COSMIC ENERGY THAT LIES DORMANT AT THE BASE OF OUR PERINEUMS. WE HAVE TO AROUSE IT, GET IT TO RISE ALONG THE ENERGY CHANNEL OF OUR SPINAL COLUMN AND PIERCE OUR VARIOUS CHAKRAS. THEN WE CAN COMMUNE WITH THE ULTIMATE UNIVERSAL SOUL!
HUH. WHEN I WANT TO COMMUNE WITH THE ULTIMATE UNIVERSAL SOUL, I PUT ON SOME ARETHA.
ARF!
grape nuts

THINK OF THE CHAKRA SYSTEM AS AN ENGINE, GINGER. IF ONE CHAKRA IS BLOCKED, THE FUEL, OR KUNDALINI, CAN'T GET THROUGH. IT'S LIKE YOU'RE NOT FIRING ON ALL YOUR CYLINDERS.
ARF!

JINGLE
SCRAPE
CLICK!
WUF!
SHH... IT'S OKAY, DIGGER. IT'S JUST LOIS DRAGGING HERSELF HOME.

HEY, DOMESTIC PARTNERS. WHUT UP?

STUART CAN'T GET HIS KUNDALINI TO RISE.
ARF!
WHERE'VE YOU BEEN? JERRY LEFT LIKE THREE MESSAGES FOR YOU YESTERDAY.
JERRY? WHAT DID HE WANT?

IT'S ON THE MACHINE. BAD NEWS ABOUT YOUR CAR. YOU HAVE A SEIZED PISTON OR SOMETHING. SHE... HE'S WAITING TO HEAR WHAT YOU WANT TO DO.
SHIT! I WAS DUE FOR AN OIL CHANGE LIKE TWO MONTHS AGO. BUT I'VE BEEN SO NERVOUS AROUND JERRY LATELY, I DIDN'T WANT TO TAKE IT IN.

NERVOUS? WHY?
I'M ATTRACTED TO HIM.

LOIS, HOW CAN YOU BE ATTRACTED TO A GAY MAN, EVEN IF HE USED TO BE A LESBIAN? I CAN'T KEEP UP.
ME NEITHER. THAT'S WHY MY PISTON SEIZED.
LOOK AT THIS. A FREE KUNDALINI CLASS!
ARF!
METRO EVENTS
SUN

"JUMP-START YOUR LIFE BY AWAKENING TO THE VIBRANT SOURCE OF COSMIC ENERGY. GENTLE INTRODUCTORY CLASS. WEAR CLOTHES YOU CAN MOVE IN."
HEALTH & FITNESS
CLOGGED ARTERIES?
NEW STUDY SHOWS DIET HIGH IN LARD TO BE BENEFICIAL

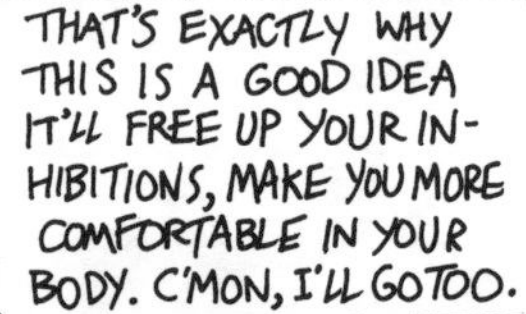
I DUNNO, SPARROW. I DON'T LIKE MOVING IN FRONT OF OTHER PEOPLE. I HAD A TRAUMATIC EXPERIENCE ONCE AT A CONTRA DANCE.
THAT'S EXACTLY WHY THIS IS A GOOD IDEA IT'LL FREE UP YOUR INHIBITIONS, MAKE YOU MORE COMFORTABLE IN YOUR BODY. C'MON, I'LL GO TOO.

KUNDALINI!
ARARAROW!

THINGS ARE AMISS AT JEZANNA'S HOUSE, TOO.
MORNING, DAD! GO AHEAD, TURN IT UP. WE'RE GONNA SLEEP IN A LITTLE MORE, BUT THE NOISE WON'T BOTHER US.
THAT'S ALL RIGHT. I'M GOING TO CHURCH.
SIDE EFFECTS ARE MILD AND MAY INCLUDE ERYSIPELAS, GANGRENE, DENGUE FEVER, TRENCH MOUTH, GONORRHEA, SHINGLES, RICKETS AND RABIES.
PARADE MAGAZINE

CHURCH? YOU DON'T GO TO CHURCH!
YOU DON'T KNOW EVERYTHING ABOUT ME, MISSY.
?
SHORTLY...
YOU'RE KINDA DRY... I THINK I MIGHT HAVE ONE OF THOSE LITTLE LUBE SAMPLES FLOATING AROUND SOMEWHERE...
I DON'T NEED LUBE! I'M PROBABLY JUST DEHYDRATED. GET ME A GLASS OF WATER.

COME ON, BABY, FACE IT.
FACE WHAT?

LATER THAT AFTERNOON...

I EXIST, SYDNEY. I TAKE UP SPACE, I MAKE NOISE. THAT'S WHAT PEOPLE DO. AND THAT'S WHY WE HAVE RELATIONSHIPS, BECAUSE WE LIKE BEING WITH PEOPLE WHO EXIST AND TAKE UP SPACE AND MAKE NOISE!
I DON'T HAVE TIME FOR THIS.
POP

THAT'S NO EXCUSE! CLARICE FINDS TIME TO BE WITH TONI **AND** TO RAISE A KID, AND HER JOB IS MUCH MORE DEMANDING THAN YOURS!
I'M GOING TO MY OFFICE NOW, BUT PLEASE CONTINUE COMPARING ME TO CLARICE-THE-SUBLIME-APOTHEOSIS-OF-FAMILY-VIRTUE AS LONG AS YOU LIKE.

WHAT'S SO BAD ABOUT BEING A FAMILY?
FAMILY IS A... A **HALLUCINATION!** A DESPERATE COMPACT PEOPLE MAKE WITH EACH OTHER TO STAVE OFF THEIR OWN GNAWING **EMPTINESS!**

CAN YOU PICK UP SOME DRANO ON YOUR WAY HOME?

MEANWHILE...
SO AT THE SAME TIME WE'VE BEEN TRYING TO RESURRECT OUR SEX LIFE WITH THESE ENFORCED DATES, WE'VE BOTH BEEN FANTASIZING ABOUT OTHER PEOPLE.
AND IT **STILL** SUCKS.

THANKS.
LET'S BE HONEST, CLARICE.

WELL... MAYBE THIS IS ALL WE CAN EXPECT AFTER BEING TOGETHER SO LONG.
BUT DON'T YOU WANT MORE THAN THAT?

WELL, SURE. BUT WHAT ARE WE GONNA DO? START SEEING OTHER WOMEN?
WELL... WE COULD START SEEING **ONE** OTHER WOMAN.

WHAT? YOU MEAN, LIKE... TOGETHER?
I KNOW YOU'VE NEVER BEEN THAT BIG ON THE IDEA...

NO, IT'S JUST... UH ... IT JUST HADN'T OCCURRED TO ME.
HAND ME THAT TEN PERCENT TRIBUNE.

YOU'RE GONNA LOOK IN THE PERSONALS?
WELL, THAT'S USUALLY WHERE THEY PUT THE ADS, ISN'T IT?
10% TRIBUNE
BUT... I MEAN... GOD! WHAT WOULD WE DO WITH RAFFI?
CLARICE, RELAX. I'M SURE WE CAN FIND SOMEONE TO WATCH HIM FOR AN HOUR.
10% TRIBUNE
DR. LAURA SPONTANEOUSLY COMBUSTS
GOD, YOU'VE GOTTA SWITCH TO DECAF. YOU KNOW, THAT THERAPIST WE SAW YEARS AGO WHEN YOU WERE SCREWING AROUND WITH GINGER.
OH. THAT WOMAN.
AN HOUR?!
FIFTY MINUTES, WHATEVER. I NEVER CAN FIGURE OUT ALL THESE LETTERS. WHAT'S LCP STAND FOR?
BODY-MIND-SPIRIT
LESBIAN CATHOLIC PROFESSIONAL?!
VERY FUNNY. TOO BAD YOU DIDN'T LIKE THAT WOMAN WE SAW BEFORE, OR I'D JUST CALL HER.
WHAT WOMAN?! WHAT ARE YOU TALKING ABOUT?!

tuesday evening...

A TIP O'THE NIB TO AMY 'TRIKONASANA' RADCLIFFE

OVER AT JEZANNA'S...
ARE YOU OKAY?
THAT CRAZY OLD COOT.

IS YOU IS, OR IS YOU AIN'T MY BABY?
PINAUD CLUB-MAN

DAD! HAVE YOU BEEN FIDDLING WITH THE THERMO-STAT AGAIN?!
NO. IT'S TWENTY-TWO DEGREES IN HERE, JUST LIKE YOU LIKE IT.

WHAT ARE YOU DOING?
DANCING A FANDANGO. WHAT'S IT LOOK LIKE I'M DOING?
CLUB MAN

WHO THE HELL IS THAT?
DING DONG!
MAYBE IT'S SOME MEAT-PACKERS LOOKING TO RENT FREEZER SPACE.

ALBERT READY?
UM...

I'M HERE TO PICK ALBERT UP.
COMING...

EUNICE, THIS IS MY DAUGHTER, ALBERTA, AND HER... ROOMMATE.
NICE TO SEE YOU AGAIN, ALBERTA.
HUH?

YOU REMEMBER EUNICE. WORKS DOWN AT THE U-HAUL, USED TO WAIT-RESS FOR ME YEARS AGO.
U-HAUL EUNICE? WHAT ARE YOU DOING HERE?
WE'RE GOING TO CHOIR PRACTICE.

HAVE A GOOD TIME.
DON'T WAIT UP.

WELL, WELL, WELL.
CAN YOU BELIEVE THAT? MY MOTH-ER'S NOT COLD IN HER GRAVE!

SUGAR, IT'S BEEN OVER TWO YEARS.
CHOIR PRAC-TICE?! THAT... THAT **JEZEBEL**!

MEANWHILE, SYDNEY'S WORKING LATE...

A TIP O' THE NIB TO HELEN SCOTT!

SHORTLY...
RING!

HELLO?
HI, SPANKY. WILL YOU BE HOME FOR DINNER?
The SINGLE VEGAN
HONEY

DINNER?! I DON'T HAVE TIME FOR DINNER! I'M COMPLETELY STUCK ON THIS ARTICLE AND NOW BETSY GILHOOLY'S GETTING PUBLISHED IN SOCIAL TEXT!
OKAY! RELAX!

IT'S NOT OKAY! I CAN'T RELAX! IF SHE GETS TENURE INSTEAD OF ME, I'LL ... I'LL ...
YOU'LL WHAT?

I'LL BE SUCKED SCREAMING INTO THE SWIRLING VOID!
SWEETIE? MAY-BE YOU'RE TRYING TOO HARD. COME ON HOME.
402
SYDNEY KRUKOWSKI

SYDNEY? HI, I'M JUST DROPPING OFF THAT RE-SEARCH YOU WANTED ON INFIDELITY STATISTICS.
OH, THANKS, OCTAVIA! THAT WAS QUICK! HEY, NICE JACKET.

THANKS! WELL, I CAN SEE YOU'RE BUSY...
WAIT, OCTAVIA! I NEED TO TALK TO YOU.
WHAT'S GOING ON? WHO'S THERE?

IT'S JUST MY GRAD ASSISTANT. LISTEN, I'M GOING TO KEEP PLOWING AWAY HERE. I'LL GET A SANDWICH OR SOMETHING.
FINE!
THOCK!
The SINGLE VEGAN
HORSE-RADISH

CLARICE AND TONI ARE HAVING THEIR THREESOME.
SO WHAT I'M HEARING FROM YOU, TONI, IS THAT YOU DON'T WANT TO DO ANYTHING TO JEOPARDIZE YOUR RELATIONSHIP.
NO, I'M COMPLETELY COMMITTED TO CLARICE.

AND CLARICE, YOUR MAIN PRIORITY IS YOUR RELATIONSHIP WITH TONI?
WELL, YEAH. I CAN'T IMAGINE LIFE WITHOUT HER.
OKAY. YOU TOLD ME, NOW TELL EACH OTHER.
SHE'S SITTING TWO INCHES AWAY. I THINK SHE PROBABLY HEARD ME.

HUMOR ME. TRY IT.
SIGH...

I CAN'T IMAGINE LIFE WITHOUT YOU.
I'M COMPLETELY COMMITTED TO YOU.

OKAY?
WELL, THAT WAS VERY NICE. BUT THE FACT STILL REMAINS, WE'RE ATTRACTED TO OTHER WOMEN.
I'M HEARING THAT THIS IS A PROBLEM FOR YOU.

MAYBE THIS WASN'T SUCH A GOOD IDEA.
IT'S NOT UNUSUAL TO FEEL ATTRACTION TO PEOPLE OTHER THAN OUR PARTNERS. IF YOU'RE SECURE IN YOUR COMMITMENT, WHY IS THAT THREATENING?

I DON'T KNOW. I JUST DON'T LIKE THE IDEA OF HER GIVING THAT KIND OF ATTENTION TO SOMEONE ELSE.
WHY NOT?
WHAT KIND OF A QUESTION IS THAT?! WOULD YOU LIKE IT?

WE HAVE A CHLD! A HOME, CAREERS. COMMUNITY WORK! THAT LIFE IS REALLY IMPORTANT TO US.
YEAH. I DON'T WANT TO WRECK ALL THAT. I MEAN, WE'VE BEEN TOGETHER LONGER THAN ANYONE ELSE WE KNOW. WE'RE AN INSTITUTION!

WHAT ARE YOU FEELING?
SAD, I GUESS. IT DOES FEEL LIKE AN INSTITUTION SOMETIMES.

IT'S LIKE CUBICLES AND INDUSTRIAL CARPETING. LIKE WE WORK FOR IT INSTEAD OF IT WORKING FOR US.
MAYBE THAT'S WHAT OUR CRUSHES ARE ABOUT. A WAY TO OPEN UP A WIN-DOW AND GET SOME AIR.

THERE ARE LOTS OF WAYS TO OPEN UP THAT WINDOW. EXPLORING YOUR ATTRAC-TIONS TO OTHER WOMEN IS ONE OPTION. BUT IT COULD ALSO BE TRAVEL, EDUCA-TION, CAREER CHANGES. THE IMPORTANT THING IS THAT YOU PAY ATTENTION TO YOUR DESIRES, THAT YOU BOTH CONTINUE TO GROW.

SO YOU'RE SAYING...
...SLEEPING WITH OTHER PEOPLE MIGHT HELP OUR RELATIONSHIP?

MEANWHILE...
GINGER, CAN YOU GIVE ME A RIDE TO RAINBOW AUTO-MOTIVE TOMORROW NIGHT TO PICK UP MY CAR?
SURE. WHEN?

ANY TIME AFTER SIX. I DON'T WANT TO RUN INTO JERRY.
LOIS, WHAT'S GOING ON?!

I DUNNO. I MEAN, I'VE BEEN REALLY GETTING INTO THIS DRAG KING STUFF... AND NOW I'M ATTRACTED TO A TRANS MAN! WHAT'S THE DEAL?! AM I A FAG?

LOIS, YOU'RE JUST YOU. SINCE WHEN ARE YOU SO HUNG UP ON TERMINOLOGY?
I KNOW. WHAT'S MY PROBLEM?

ANYHOW, JERRY LIKES GUYS. IT'S NOT LIKE ANY-THING'S GONNA HAPPEN.
THAT'S MY PROBLEM.

@APRÈS YOGA...
I'VE NEVER BEEN SO HUMILIATED IN MY LIFE!
STUART, WHAT WAS I SUPPOSED TO DO? SAY NO, I CAN'T DO THIS STRETCH WITH YOU BECAUSE MY BOYFRIEND'S SECOND CHAKRA IS BLOCKED?
260
The YOGA PLACE
I DON'T MEAN JUNE. I MEAN WHEN THE INSTRUCTOR WAS USING ME TO DEMONSTRATE THE WRONG WAY TO DO DOWNWARD DOG AND MY TIGHTS RIPPED!
NOBODY NOTICED THAT! YOU'RE SO SELF-CONSCIOUS!
EXIT
YEAH.
EV-RY BODY WANTS
TO BE SOMEBODY!
NOBODY NOTICED. THAT'S WHY MR. SWEATPANTS SAID, "DUDE, HOW DO YOU GET YOUR WHITES SO WHITE?"
HEY, LOOK. THIS PLACE DOES CHAKRA BALANCING.
AWAKENINGS
CHAKRA BALANCING
AURA CLEANSING
REIKI
TAX PREP
HUH. COOL.
MAYBE YOU SHOULD CHECK IT OUT.
SPIN CYCLE
SPIN CYCLE
BEGINNERS CLASS
FRIDAYS 7 PM
SCHWEIN

friday night...

BABY, MOVE ON. YOUR DAD HAS.
GOD! IT'S LIKE A STEAMBATH IN HERE! I'VE GOTTA CHANGE.
DING DONG!

COME ON IN, EUNICE.
HOPE YOU LIKE RED. IT WAS ON SALE.
CHILLABLE RED
5 LITERS

MEANWHILE, AT MO'S...
MAY
RUCK
RUCK

AND AT THE UNIVERSITY...
WHUMP
COMING OF AGE IN SAMOA
PSYCHOPATHIA SEXUALIS
LITTLE WOMEN

SYDNEY?! I SAW YOUR LIGHT ON! THOUGHT I'D STOP IN AND SEE IF YOU NEEDED ANYTHING.
OH, HI, OCTAVIA.
NO!
402
SYDNEY KRUKOWSKI

HOW'S THE ARTICLE COMING?
I'M AFRAID IT ISN'T. I CAN'T SEEM TO FOCUS MY ARGUMENT.

DO YOU WANT TO RUN ANYTHING BY ME? I'D LOVE TO HEAR IT.
ALL I'VE GOT SO FAR IS THE TITLE, "THE POLYAMOROUS CRITIC; PLURALISM, PROMISCUITY AND MULTIPLE ORGANONS."

HMM. WOW. I LIKE IT. IT'S SO LIBIDINAL, BUT IN A LIMINAL KIND OF WAY. YOU'VE DEFINITELY GOT MY INTEREST.
REALLY?
iJac

ABSOLUTELY. SO WHAT'S THE PROBLEM?
I DON'T KNOW. IT'S LIKE I'M COMPLETELY DRY.
iLac

RUN YOUR PROPOSITION BY ME. MAYBE AS YOU TALK, IT'LL START TO COME.
WELL... I'M USING POLYAMORY AS A METAPHOR TO SHOW HOW AUTHENTIC CRITICAL DETACHMENT CAN ONLY BE ATTAINED BY EMBRACING ALL POSSIBLE POSITIONS WITH EQUAL ABANDON...
iMack

BUT I DON'T KNOW WHERE TO START. THEORETICALLY, OF COURSE, I'D START EVERYWHERE AT ONCE.
MMM. YES, THAT WOULD BE IDEAL. MAYBE YOU'LL JUST HAVE TO CLOSE YOUR EYES AND PLUNGE IN SOMEWHERE.
PERHAPS YOU'RE RIGHT.
ELSEWHERE...
I TOLD YOU THAT WAS A SLIPPERY SLOPE, VANESSA.
LAPLAPLAPLAP

MEANWHILE...
" SEE THE BALL PYTHON TIG..."
TIGHTEN.
"... TIGHTEN AROUND ITS PREY UNTIL IT STOPS BREATHING. SNAKES ARE OUR FRIENDS. THEY ARE PART OF THE BALANCE OF NATURE. SOME SNAKES MAKE GOOD PETS. THEY ARE CLEAN AND EASY TO TAKE CARE OF."

SHORTLY...
SO... ARE WE CRAZY TO BE CONSIDERING THIS?
TONI, YOU KNOW I'M TERRIFIED OF SNAKES!

I MEANT THE OTHER THING. WHAT WE TALKED ABOUT IN THERAPY.
THAT WE SHOULD HAVE SEX WITH OTHER PEOPLE? IT'S THAT THERAPIST WHO'S CRAZY.

I KNOW. IT'S ABSURD. IT'S IRRESPONSIBLE. IT'S TOO RISKY.
WE'RE A FAMILY!

WE'LL GET OVER THESE CRUSHES. IT'S JUST SOME KIND OF PHASE.
RIGHT. BESIDES, WHAT WOULD COMMITMENT MEAN IF YOU WERE IN A RELATIONSHIP WHERE YOU COULD DO WHATEVER YOU FELT LIKE?

IF THERE ARE NO LIMITS, IF THERE'S NOTHING HOLDING YOU THERE, YOU MIGHT AS WELL BE, LIKE...

FREE?

MEANWHILE...
THANKS FOR THE LIFT, GINGER. ARE YOU SURE YOU DON'T WANT TO COME TO THE DRAG KING SHOW? MAX AXEL'S BECOMING SOMETHING OF A LOCAL LEGEND.
TEMPTING, BUT IT'S BEEN A LONG WEEK. I'LL WAIT TO MAKE SURE YOUR CAR STARTS.
RAINBOW AUTOMOTIVE
RAINBOW AUTO

HEY!
JERRY! HI.
NOK NOK

RAINBOW Automotive
UH... IT'S OKAY. GO AHEAD.
HAVE FUN.
Castrol

I WAS WORKING LATE ON A VALVE JOB. COME ON IN. YOUR CAR'S IN THE BAY.
RAINBOW AUTOMOTIVE

SO. YOU'RE MAX TONIGHT.
YEAH, UM... THERE'S A SHOW DOWN AT CLUB L. JEEZ, I HOPE YOU'RE NOT INSULTED THAT I'M PLAYING AROUND LIKE THIS. I MEAN, I KNOW YOUR MUSTACHE DOESN'T PEEL OFF.
Castrol
Max
Jerry
STP

LOIS, RELAX. IF IT BOTHERED ME, I WOULDN'T HAVE GIVEN YOU THAT UNIFORM.
OH. RIGHT.

YOU LOOK PRETTY GOOD IN IT.
REALLY?
CASTROL

WHAT TIME DOES THE SHOW START? ARE YOU IN A RUSH?
UH... NO RUSH, WHY?

WANNA FOOL AROUND?
UH... WHAT DO YOU MEAN, EXACTLY?
Max

I THINK YOU KNOW WHAT I MEAN, EXACTLY...
MAX.
WHOA! HEH HEH...
Labor Rate
$42/HR
WITH OWN PARTS
$50/HR
STP

JERRY! DUDE... UH.. YOU KNOW IT'S JUST RUBBER. IT'S NOT EVEN HARD, IT'S MY "MR. SOFTIE."
HE FEELS FINE TO ME. I JUST HAD MY T SHOT THIS MORNING AND I'M HORNY AS HELL.

OH, MAN.
CUTE. IS THIS JUST AN EXTRA REALISTIC TOUCH, OR COULDN'T YOU AFFORD THE LARGE MODEL?
ZIP

MEANWHILE, IN THE GROOVE OF ACADEME...
BETTER?
OH, YEAH. MY HEADACHE'S PRACTICALLY GONE.
iMac

SO YOU REALLY THINK POLYAMORY IS AN ACCURATE TROPE FOR THE APPROACH I'M TRYING TO DESCRIBE?
Y'KNOW, THE THING ABOUT POLYAMORY IS, IT ONLY WORKS IF YOU'RE HONEST. EVERYONE NEEDS TO KNOW WHERE THEY STAND. MAYBE YOU'RE STUCK BECAUSE YOU'RE NOT BEING COMPLETELY HONEST.

LIKE, MY PRIMARY GIRLFRIEND HAS REALLY BEEN BUGGING ABOUT THE TIME I SPEND WITH YOU. AND AS WE TALKED ABOUT IT I HAD TO ADMIT THAT YEAH, I WAS INTERESTED IN BEING MORE THAN YOUR GRAD ASSISTANT.
AND WHAT DID SHE SAY?
iMac

WELL, SHE WASN'T ECSTATIC OR ANYTHING. BUT SHE FELT BETTER KNOWING WHAT WAS GOING ON.
OCTAVIA, YOU'RE A GENIUS!

SMACK

SEE YOU MONDAY!

STUART'S GOING FOR A SPIN...
FIRST TIME?
Y-YES.
SPIN CYCLE
SPINNER
SPIN CYCLE
SPIN-O-MATIC

BACK AT TH' RANCH...
SURE, JIM. WE'D BE HAPPY TO. GO AHEAD AND GIVE HER OUR NUMBER.
YEAH. I'LL SEE YOU AT THE ROTARY CLUB THING.
ORGANIC SKETTI SAUCE
COUS COUS
GOYA
HOROSCOPE

DON'T TELL ME. WE'RE ABOUT TO BE THE LESBIAN POSTER FAMILY AGAIN.

I FIGURED IT WAS OKAY WITH YOU. THE DAILY DISTRESS IS LOOKING FOR PEOPLE TO INTERVIEW FOR A FEATURE ON LESBIANS AND GAY MEN RAISING KIDS. YOU KNOW, HOW IT'S JUST AS IF WE WERE HUMAN.
SURE. OKAY, WHERE WERE WE?
RAFFI

WE EACH GET ONE DAY A MONTH TO GO DO WHATEVER WE WANT. NO QUESTIONS ASKED.
OKAY. BUT WHAT IF THERE WAS SOME KIND OF CRISIS HERE. WE'D HAVE TO KNOW WHERE EACH OTHER WAS.
RAFFI

PAGER.
BRILLIANT.
RAFFI
R

WHICH BRINGS US TO THE NEXT POINT. WHOEVER WE MIGHT HAPPEN TO BE WITH HAS TO UNDERSTAND THAT **OUR** RELATIONSHIP COMES FIRST.
RIGHT. COMPLETE HONESTY WITH ALL POTENTIAL PARTIES.
BUT NOT NECESSARILY WITH EACH OTHER. BASIC HONESTY IS GOOD, BUT I DON'T KNOW IF I'D WANT THE DETAILED REPORT.
ME EITHER. HONESTY ON A NEED TO KNOW BASIS.
I CAN'T BELIEVE WE'RE ACTUALLY HAVING THIS DISCUSSION.
THAT'S ALL IT IS. A DISCUSSION. WE'RE JUST TRYING OUT THE IDEA.
WHAT WOULD THE **DISTRESS** REPORTER THINK?
WOULDN'T **THAT** THROW A WRENCH INTO HER STORY.
HUH. I HAVEN'T FELT LIKE THIS IN A WHILE.
MMM. YOU KNOW WHAT I'D LIKE RIGHT NOW?

SOME OF THOSE TOASTER WAFFLES WITH ICE CREAM AND WARM MAPLE SYRUP.
TOASTER WAFFLES WITH ICE CREAM AND WARM MAPLE SYRUP?

THAT SOUNDS VERY MESSY.
OH, IT WILL BE.

DESSERT? ALBERT, I COULDN'T EAT ANOTHER BITE!
'COURSE YOU CAN. IT'S MY SPECIAL APPLE PIE.
IT'S A LITTLE CLOSE IN HERE. I'M GONNA OPEN THE WINDOW A CRACK.

GIRL, YOU NEED TO GET YOURSELF ONE OF THOSE LITTLE BATTERY OPERATED FANS. JUST TAKE IT OUT WHEN YOU FEEL A HOT FLASH COMING ON. I DON'T KNOW HOW I'D A GOT THROUGH THE CHANGE WITHOUT ONE.

EXCUSE ME?
BE RIGHT BACK, LADIES. NATURE CALLING.

I'M NOT HAVING HOT FLASHES, AND I DON'T NEED ADVICE.

I CAN TELL YOU DON'T MUCH CARE FOR ME, ALBERTA.
JEZANNA.

JEZANNA. BUT THERE'S NO CALL TO BE SO MEAN. I DON'T KNOW WHERE YOU GET IT. YOUR FATHER'S A PERFECT GENTLE-MAN AND I NEVER MET A NICER LADY THAN YOUR MAMA.
YOU KNEW MY MOTHER?
SHE WHO MUST BE OBEYED

'COURSE I DID. SHE CAME INTO THE DINER ALMOST EVERY DAY WHEN I WORKED FOR ALBERT.
IF YOU REALLY KNEW MY MOTH-ER, YOU'D KNOW SHE WAS NOT A NICE LADY.

OH, SHE SPOKE HER MIND. BUT THAT JUST MEANT YOU COULD BELIEVE WHAT SHE SAID. LORD, SHE WAS PROUD OF YOU.
She WHO MUST BE OBEYED

YOU WERE JUST STARTING UP YOUR BOOKSTORE BACK THEN. SHE'D TELL ME ALL ABOUT HOW GLAD SHE WAS YOU GOT YOUR BUSINESS SENSE FROM HER AND NOT YOUR DADDY.
SHE ALWAYS TOLD ME I WAS A FOOL TO OPEN MADWIMMIN. SHE SAID, "YOU GOT THE NAME RIGHT, AT LEAST."

I'M JUST TELLING YOU WHAT SHE TOLD ME... AND ANYONE ELSE WHO'D LISTEN.
SNIFF.

FLICK
GURGLE

QUILTING
EXHIBIT

YOU DIDN'T HAVE TO WAIT FOR ME! GO ON, EAT YOUR PIE! THE ICE CREAM'S MELTING.
ICE CREAM
SHE WHO MUST

MO! MO, I'M HOME!

MO, I JUST HAD A BREAKTHROUGH ABOUT THIS WHOLE POLYAMORY THING!
I'M SURE **THEORETICAL CRITIQUES OF CRITICAL THEORY** WILL BE VERY IMPRESSED.

NO, NOT ABOUT THE ARTICLE! ABOUT MY LIFE! ABOUT US! I'M GIDDY AS A SCHOOLGIRL!
IF THIS INVOLVES ANY ACTUAL SCHOOLGIRLS, SYDNEY, I'M OUTTA HERE.

MO, I HAVEN'T BEEN HONEST WITH YOU. I'VE BEEN TALKING FOR MONTHS ABOUT HOW I WANT US TO OPEN UP OUR RELATIONSHIP... BUT THE TRUTH IS, I ALREADY HAVE! YOU'RE NOT MY PRIMARY PARTNER!

MY WORK IS!

YOU'RE LIKE, THE OTHER WOMAN! THAT'S WHY I'VE HAD SUCH TROUBLE BEING THERE FOR YOU! IT FELT LIKE BETRAYING MY WORK! BUT NOW THAT I'VE FACED THE TRUTH ABOUT WHAT'S GOING ON, I CAN COMMIT!
I'M THE OTHER WOMAN?

I'M ALL YOURS! WELL, 48 PERCENT OR SO, ANYWAY.
GOD, SYDNEY. YOU WEAR ME OUT.

I'M SORRY. YOU NEED TIME TO GET USED TO THE IDEA. IT MUST BE SOMEWHAT OF A SHOCK.

ACTUALLY, IT'S NOT. IT MAKES SENSE. I GUESS I'VE ALWAYS KNOWN, ON SOME LEVEL. IT'S A RELIEF TO HEAR YOU ADMIT IT.
I BROUGHT YOU SOMETHING!
ACE HARDWARE

SHALL WE?

WHAT ABOUT YOUR ARTICLE?
FUCK MY ARTICLE.
Sklorp!

MEANWHILE...
RAINBOW AUTOMOTIVE
RAINBOW AUTO
OHHH!

Max
OHHH, MANNN!

WORLD'S BEST VANILLA
FANNING the ASHES
MAPLE SYRUP GRADE A

R-E-S-P-E-C-T! FIND OUT WHAT IT MEANS TO ME!
SOCK IT TO ME! SOCK IT TO ME! SOCK IT TO ME! SOCK IT TO ME!
SCHWEIN
SPINNER

I CAN JUST SUBMIT THE ARTICLE FOR THE NEXT ISSUE. I'VE GOT A WHOLE NEW TAKE ON IT NOW, ANYWAY. WHAT WAS I THINKING? CAN ONE POSSIBLY ACHIEVE AUTHENTIC CRITICAL DETACHMENT UNLESS ONE IS CRITICALLY **ENGAGED?** I DON'T THINK SO!

I'VE ALWAYS WANTED TO BE THE OTHER WOMAN.
Glorp

GOD, THAT WAS WILD! I MEAN, I'VE COME FROM BLOWJOBS BEFORE, BUT IT WAS ALWAYS MORE... CONCEPTUAL. THIS WAS LIKE YOU WERE SUCKING MY DICK! MY ACTUAL DICK!
I'VE ALWAYS BEEN HANDY WITH TOOLS.
Strap-on Tools

SO, UH... DO YOU WANNA GO SOMEPLACE LESS LIKE THE SET OF A PORN MOVIE?

I DON'T THINK SO. THIS IS NICE, BUT YOU'RE NOT EXACTLY MY TYPE, YOU KNOW.
YEAH. TOO BAD I'M NOT A BOY, OR YOU'RE NOT A GIRL.
THE PROFESSIONAL
BRAKE SERVICE

HEY, YOU HAD YOUR CHANCE. I'VE BEEN RE-PAIRING THIS CAR OF YOURS FOR TEN YEARS AND YOU NEVER GAVE ME A SECOND LOOK WHEN I WAS GERALDINE.
YOU WERE WAY TOO BUTCH FOR ME THEN, DUDE.

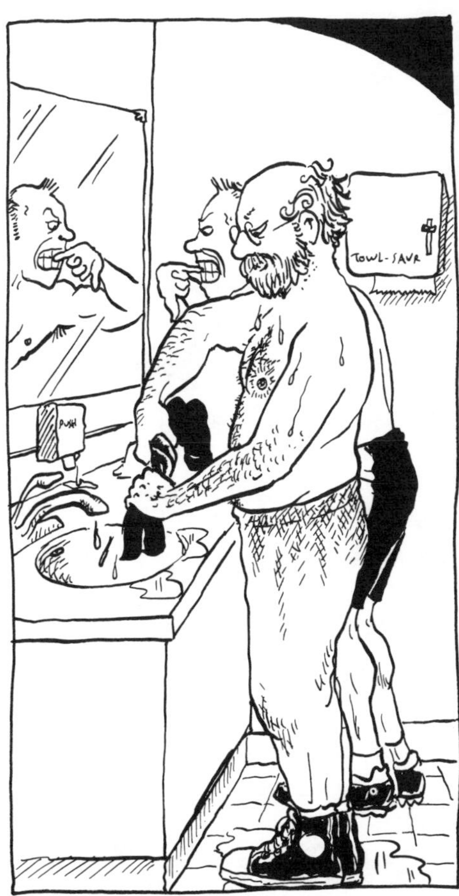
TOWL-SAVR
PUSH

I DARESAY THERE WAS NO FANTASIZING ABOUT GLORIA **THIS** TIME.
NO, BUT I HAD QUITE AN ELABORATE SCENARIO GOING ABOUT OUR THERAPIST.

GOD. THESE THINGS REALLY WORK.
WHO KNEW?
SSSLORP!

the next morning...

WOW.
UNH.

YOUR AURA IS **HUGE**.
YOU'RE GIVING OFF SUCH INTENSE VIBRATIONS!

I THINK WE CAN TURN IT OFF NOW.
OH, RIGHT.
BZZZZZZZ

IT'S A QUARTER TO NINE ALREADY?!
RELAX! IT'S SATURDAY. REMEMBER?
TROJAN
VERY SENSITIVE

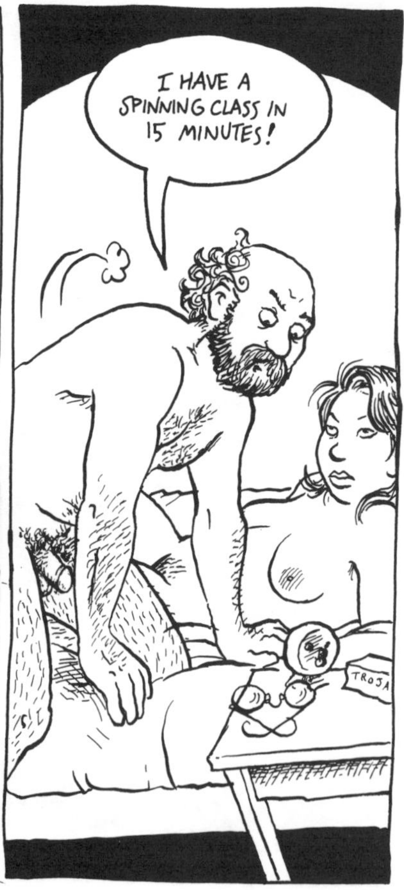
I HAVE A SPINNING CLASS IN 15 MINUTES!

AT MO AND SYDNEY'S...
WHAT ARE YOU DOING?
WAITING FOR YOU TO GET UP SO I CAN START VACUUMING. AND I WAS HOPING YOU COULD HELP ME HAUL OUT THE RECYCLING BEFORE YOU LEFT FOR WORK.
HEY, I'M THE FLING. GET YOUR PRIMARY PARTNER TO DO THAT STUFF. WE'RE JUST SUPPOSED TO SHARE EXALTED MOMENTS OF SEXUAL TRANSCENDENCE, COMPLETELY OBLIVIOUS TO THE MUNDANE EXIGENCIES OF DAILY LIFE.
BLEAK HOUSE
COME BACK TO BED.
WHAT DO YOU WANT? TRANSCENDENCE OR TIDINESS?
CULTURE IS ORDINARY
THE VACUUM CLEANER BAG'S FULL... LEMME CHECK IF THERE'S A NEW ONE UNDER THE SINK.

HEY, I'M HUNGRY! I THOUGHT WE WERE GONNA HAVE BREAKFAST BEFORE YOU OPENED UP.
I'M NOT OPENING UP YET. I JUST WANNA DO SOMETHING BEFORE ANYONE ELSE GETS HERE.
ACME AWNING
MADWIMMIN BOOKS
CLICK

WHAT? ARE YOU EMBEZZLING FROM YOURSELF?
SORT OF. I'VE GIVEN LOIS SO MUCH SHIT FOR TAKING OVER THE STORE WITH THIS STUFF...
OURSELVE GROWING BOLDER

I'D NEVER HEAR THE END OF IT IF SHE CAUGHT ME SHOPPING FOR SOME.
LUBRICANTS
PROBE

I'VE ALWAYS BEEN CURIOUS ABOUT THIS CURRIED EGG-PLANT FLAVOR.
DOES THIS MEAN WE'RE GRACEFULLY ACCEPTING REALITY?

WELL, LIKE MY MAMA ALWAYS SAID, GO WITH THE FLOW, OR EAT SOME CROW.
SMART WOMAN.
GOOP
VISCOUS SILK
ASTRO SLIDE
FAMILY SIZE

SO SHOULD WE GET A BOTTLE FOR YOUR DAD AND EUNICE, TOO?
AS SHE ALSO USED TO SAY, GIRL, DON'T PUSH ME.
SELF-HELP

HEY! YOUR CAR'S FIXED.
LIKE NEW.

THAT JERRY'S A MAGICIAN.
YEP.

HI!
WUF!

WHAT ARE ALL THOSE BAGS? YOU NEVER GO SHOPPING!
GIVE ME A COUPLE MINUTES AND I'LL SHOW YOU.

WAIT, D'YOU HAVE ANY LAUNDRY? I'M DOING A DARK LOAD.
OH, YEAH. HERE.

DON'T GO ANYWHERE! I'LL BE RIGHT BACK!

SO HOW WAS THE SHOW LAST NIGHT?
GREAT! I'M THE REIGNING KING.

"BEST LEAGUE AVERAGE, 1978?"
I GAVE AN INSPIRED PERFORMANCE.

YEAH? AND WHERE DID YOU SPEND THE NIGHT, MAX? THAT 'STACHE IS LOOKING A LITTLE THE WORSE FOR WEAR.
WITH THE RUNNER-UP.

OH. I THOUGHT MAYBE YOU MANAGED TO SEDUCE JERRY.
UH... NOT EXACTLY.

WHAT DO YOU MEAN, NOT EXACTLY?! I WAS JUST KIDDING! DID SOMETHING HAPPEN?
LET'S JUST SAY I LEARNED A THING OR TWO ABOUT THE FINER POINTS OF INTERNAL COMBUSTION.
WUF!

SHORTLY...
WOW. YOU'RE SO, UH... COLOR-FUL.
IT'S OPTIC YELLOW. IT MAKES YOU REALLY VISIBLE TO CARS.
YEAH, I'VE HEARD YOU CAN GET INTO SOME PRETTY HEAVY TRAFFIC ON THOSE INDOOR STATIONARY BIKES.
I THINK YOU LOOK GREAT, STU.
THANK YOU, LOIS.
NICE PACKAGE, TOO.
BUT I DON'T KNOW HOW YOU GUYS STAND HAVING THESE THINGS PERMANENTLY ATTACHED.

that evening...

RAFFI! I THOUGHT YOU SAID THIS THING ATE MICE!
HELP! HE'S EATING ME!
THANKS, SYDNEY. WE ALWAYS LIKE TO WORK HIM INTO A LATHER RIGHT AROUND BEDTIME.
RAFFI, COME ON UPSTAIRS.
NOOO! I WANNA PLAY WITH SYDNEY!
©A BIT LATER...
IT'S NICE TO SEE YOU TWO. I THOUGHT YOU WEREN'T GONNA BE ABLE TO COME BECAUSE OF YOUR WORK, SYDNEY.
WELL, I HAD A LITTLE REALIZATION ABOUT MY WORK.
IT'S HER PRIMARY RELATIONSHIP. I'M THE MISTRESS.
IRONICALLY, IT WAS ONLY BY ACKNOWLEDGING THIS THAT I FIND MYSELF ABLE TO FINALLY COMMIT TO BEING WITH MO EXCLUSIVELY.
HUH.
SHE'S ALWAYS BEEN CYNICAL ABOUT MONOGAMY, BUT NOW SHE'S GAINING AN APPRECIATION OF ITS DECEPTIVELY SIMPLE ELEGANCE.

COMMITTING TO ONE PERSON IS LIKE... IS LIKE EATING A SUPER PREMIUM VANILLA ICE CREAM...
UH... THIS SEEMS TO HAVE MELTED AND REFROZEN.
WORLD'S BEST VANILLA
... THE LACK OF DISTRACTION YIELDS LAYERS OF RICHNESS AND NUANCE THAT THE MORE INDISCRIMINATE CHUNKY MONKEY*, FOR EXAMPLE, COULD NEVER HOPE TO APPROXIMATE.
BESIDES, WHAT WOULD COMMITMENT MEAN IF YOU WERE IN A RELATIONSHIP WHERE YOU COULD DO WHATEVER YOU FELT LIKE?
EXACTLY. IF THERE ARE NO LIMITS, IT'S **CHAOS**. TO EXPERIENCE TRUE FREEDOM, SOME ORDERING FORCE IS NECESSARY.
NOW WITH SLIM-FAST!
* NO COMPENSATION WAS RECEIVED FOR THIS EGREGIOUS PRODUCT PLACEMENT.

YOU TWO ARE A REAL INSPIRATION, YOU KNOW. ALL THESE YEARS...
YOU'RE AN INSTITUTION.

LATER...
SEE YA.
DRIVE SAFE.

AH, YOUTH.
SHOULD WE HAVE TOLD THEM?

THAT WE'RE THINKING OF BECOMING SUBURBAN SWINGERS? NO, LET THEM DREAM.
MOMENTARILY...
I LOVE VISITING THOSE GUYS. WE SHOULD THINK ABOUT BUYING A HOUSE.
Y'KNOW, THAT ICE CREAM ANALOGY COULD BE THE PERFECT DISCURSIVE MOTIF TO TIE MY ARTICLE TOGETHER. YOU GO ON TO BED. I'M GONNA MAKE A FEW NOTES.